D1622537

themondaymemo.com

By

Daniel S. Wolgemuth

Honor Books

Tulsa, Oklahoma

themondaymemo.com:

ISBN 1-56292-748-5

Copyright © 2000 by Daniel S.Wolgemuth

Published by Honor Books

P.O. Box 55388

Tulsa, Oklahoma 74155

To Mary,
my Monday Memo
personified.
I love you.

Acknowledgements

Where do I start? Off and on for more than fifteen years, I have been capturing the people in my life in story form. As a result, the acknowledgements for this book are spread throughout the pages that follow. The names you'll read are real. They're my family, my friends, my coworkers, my neighbors, and sometimes perfect strangers. It is their contribution to my life that has helped to germinate this idea. It is their investment in a moment or an hour or a lifetime that has shaped the unfolding stories of life for me. They have been my inspiration. I will indeed acknowledge them, but in context, mid-story, with a full and grateful heart. You know who you are. Find your pages, dog-ear them, and consider them my tribute to you. Thanks for giving me something worth writing about.

There are a few names that need special recognition. My wife Mary, my children, Andrew, Erik, and Alli. You believed so much that you made me believe. My brother Ken, who not only believed but promoted. You're amazing. To the two families that stand at my side, the Wolgemuths and the Cargos, thanks. I am so blessed. To the people at MSL, Crown, Frankona, and ERC. You made it worth writing each week. To the incredible team at Honor Books, especially Rebecca Currington and Mark Gilroy. You guys made this process so much fun.

Finally, to my parents, Sam and Grace, and Don and Eunice, the first by birth, the second by marriage. You have multiplied every joy and shared every burden. You have been an inspiration beyond words.

Bless you.

Introduction

I stepped onto the elevator of my hotel, pulling a suitcase with a computer bag balanced on the top. I had a meeting across town, and before that, I needed to check out of my hotel, call for a taxi, and ride to the office. I'd slept poorly the night before, a problem I often have on the second night of an international trip.

During the moments that it took for my three-floor journey, I glanced up long enough to catch an unguarded glimpse of myself in the smoked mirrors that formed the wall covering of the elevator. It was that glimpse, that moment that showed me what others would soon be seeing. This was not the kind of rehearsed look I had gotten in room 207 just a few minutes before. This was spontaneous and honest, and it told me more than the thirty minutes I'd spent dressing for my day.

I believe stories are just those glimpses—private, unguarded looks at myself, reflected off of the people and experiences of everyday life. Not posed, but candid. Not arranged, but spontaneous.

This is a book about those glimpses. Images that I've written about on Mondays for roughly fifteen years. They're unguarded, honest, and telling, but they're also heartwarming, challenging, and motivational.

Read a couple. See if you catch a candid glimpse of yourself—a quick image that tells you more than the hours of feedback you get in prearranged moments. You'll know these stories. They could be yours. You'll nod and smile and relate. That's *themondaymemo.com*. A book of mirrors placed strategically throughout your life. A book that is intended to help reveal as well as entertain.

Catch a glimpse. It might just be someone you recognize.

D S Wolgemuth

1999

Mondays Happen

It was a good landing. We rolled along the tarmac and then sat motionless as the pilot waited for a gate to become available. Anxious to get to my destination, I gazed out the window, hoping we'd soon be rolling. Our spot in line was immediately adjacent to the main Detroit runway, so I had a clear view of the incoming planes making their first contact with earth—the spot where the concrete of the runway has been blackened by rubber tires.

The exact location of the touchdown varied somewhat, according to the size and speed of the aircraft, but one thing remained constant. When the wheels touched the runway, a burst of white smoke appeared. As I watched, each metal bird produced a similar plume.

Understanding this phenomenon is not particularly difficult. It is the result of the considerable speed still propelling the plane and the motionless tires hitting the firm, smooth, unforgiving pavement. Upon impact, the tires skid for a moment before beginning to rotate, and the skidding produces smoke. Yet the wheels quickly catch up, performing the task for which they were designed. The smoke is not a sign of trouble. It is simply part of the process.

That plume of smoke reminds me of the moment when our own wheels, idle from the weekend, encounter the concrete of Monday morning and we must suddenly spin into action. Monday morning, that is when we come smack up against reality and responsibility.

Regardless of who you are or what your position in life might be, Mondays happen. Parents, students, employers, employees, friends, teachers—people in all walks of life must face the realities of Monday morning. That is the reason I have chosen to write to you at this particular time in the week. I want to give you something encouraging to get you through that initial skid, that moment when your wheels touch the ground and the plume of white smoke appears. Something to help your wheels start rolling along at full speed. May God go with you wherever your journey may take you.

Have a great week.

"e" versus "u"

Greetings to you this Monday morning.

Without a doubt the "e"-revolution has hit. The face of international business is changing to meet the demand, opportunity, and competition revolving around electronic commerce. From life insurance to computers to airline tickets, transactions across the Internet are rapidly replacing traditional distribution channels. Call it "e"-commerce, "e"-business, or virtual corporations, we are on a fast track to replacing mouths with modems and handshakes with encrypted transactions.

Over the weekend, I browsed the web looking for a vacation spot seven hundred miles from home. I had a short "chat" with a friend who was on-line at the same time I was, and I received the regular glut of daily e-mail. I'm doing my best to exploit this new technology whenever possible. In fact, on a recent trip to the East Coast, I observed with interest the number of people around me who in some manner where doing the same. Presentations were being prepared and reviewed on how to make the most of the "e"-commerce environment. We've clearly turned the "e"-corner and we'll never go back.

Between Chicago and Hartford, I had my laptop out, working at "e"-speed. A mental lapse forced me to pull out my planner and review a note I had written to myself earlier in the day. When I did so, some index cards slipped out of the inside pocket of my leather binder. The cards, simple white, lined sheets, had been given to me by my family with Father's Day wishes scrawled on them. There was nothing "e" about these letters—no graphics, no sounds, no tech, no font, just real ink, real paper, and real handwriting. They were neither spell-checked nor templated, but they screamed at me with a voice that far exceeded my fifty unread messages and the slick presentations on which I was working. I sat and read each one ... again. I cherish them. They're rough but they're real.

I believe in "e." It's here to stay, and I'm thrilled with the possibilities. Yet the greatest disservice we could do to this new revolution is to think that "e" could replace "u." There is no bandwidth wide enough for relationship.

"E" isn't everything. Sometime this week, write a real letter and lick a stamp. You'll be amazed at what thirty-three cents can buy.

Have a great week.

4 by 100

Few people would dispute that the performance of runner extraordinaire Michael Johnson at the Atlanta Olympics amounted to an historic event. While setting an Olympic record in the 400-meter and shattering his own world record in the 200-meter, he became the first man ever to win both events in the same Olympic games. His style, strength, endurance, and concentration have distinguished him worldwide as one of our planet's finest athletes, an individual of significant talent, performing on a global stage with show-stopping results.

Also of particular interest in Atlanta was the 4-by-100-meter relay. This is a race in which four individuals cover a single lap around the track, each contributing a quarter of the distance. The combination of speed, coordination, and timing makes this an exceptionally exciting event to observe.

As I sat at home watching, I couldn't help but consider what a remarkable demonstration of individual versus team accomplishment these events provided. While Michael Johnson, the winner of fifty-five consecutive 400-meter finals, performed as one of the best ever at this single-lap distance, he proved no match for the collective efforts of four less accomplished team members. In spite of his dominance in the individual distance, his times fade into oblivion when compared to the time required for four individuals to cover the same distance in a relay manner. In fact, both the men's and women's teams outperformed the master individual champion.

With resounding clarity, the value of teamwork rings from the Olympic oval. While individual accomplishment should never be overlooked, it is a poor match for a tightly unified, commonly committed team.

Teamwork is about sharing the load—a way of accomplishing what individually is beyond reach. My goal is to stop running the race alone—to grab firmly the baton and seek a teammate to hand it to. I want to spend more time working on my hand-off than on my endurance. I want to contribute to the one-lap distance, while concerning myself with my one-hundred meters. I want to embrace teamwork because, above all, it works.

Call it family, call it friends, use it in the workplace, practice it in life.

Have a great week.

Build, Race, Improve

Alli's package contained a rectangular block of wood, four black plastic wheels, four shiny chrome axles, and a few decals—the raw materials for an annual pinewood derby racer. At our previous derby, Alli and I had been content to make it down the course without losing a wheel, but we had vowed to make our next entry a winner.

That pledge translated into a considerable amount of work. But slowly, our racer began to take shape, as we cut and sanded the wood, carved grooves, and applied the paint. Then we turned our attention to performance. We worked to ensure that the wheels could rotate without restriction and that the total weight of the model was as close to five ounces as possible.

The night before the big race, we went down to the track for an unofficial weigh-in and test drive. We set the shiny black racecar on the small electronic scale, and cheered as the display flashed up 5.0! Next, we positioned our racer on one of the inside lanes, and when the gate dropped, we easily beat our three competitors. We set the car on the track for a rerun, and once again, its performance exceeded our expectation. We quickly retrieved our racer and held it protectively while our competitors immediately began to work on wheels and weight.

Back at home, I made sure that Alli set the racer up where it would be safe and the next day on the way to the track, I had her hold it tenderly, careful not to disturb the wheels. We checked in and made a couple of preliminary runs. As anticipated, our little black car won both races, but certainly not by the overwhelming margins we had witnessed the night before. At race time, Alli ran in the second heat, and to our horror and disbelief, we finished last. Subsequent races brought more of the same. I was baffled. Ultimately, the second-place finisher for the day was a car we had easily beaten during the prelims. While we were obsessed with protecting our racer, the other competitors were concentrating on improvement. Yesterday's results made us satisfied. We thought we had enough for race day.

Losers are content to stay where they are today. They clutch their skills tightly while others lubricate, adjust, and redesign theirs. On race day, their preliminary speed is the best they can hope for, and sometimes that's simply not enough. Build, race, improve, then race again.

Have a great week.

Curbs

Greetings to you
this Monday morning.

Approximately one mile from my house are several acres of open farmland. Over the five years that we've lived in the Kansas City area, we've regularly observed cattle grazing on the gently rolling hills that mark the terrain of this farm lot. That is until several months ago when the bulls were replaced by bulldozers, and grazing gave way to grating.

During those months, I watched with interest as enormous vehicles shaped, carved, dug, and contoured the land, all the while keeping the ultimate purpose for the earthen asset a secret.

Last week the mystery was solved. As if a seamstress had lain a pattern on top of rich black satin, construction crews outlined their design with … curbs. For days on end, unfettered power had characterized the activity. Now almost overnight, simple white bands of concrete define streets, cul-de-sacs, and driveway insets, replacing the openness with unpretentious boundaries—boundaries that shine light on the engineer's plan and ignite the developer's dream. Boundaries that turn a field into a neighborhood.

Boundaries get a bad rap these days. They're considered confining and restrictive. Yet, viewed in the proper context, boundaries define the perimeters, giving builders the freedom to create and the confidence to begin construction. They also provide consistency. For years to come, circumstances, situations, conditions, and even residents will come and go, but the lines drawn this past week will likely stay the same.

Across the landscape of daily life, we are confronted with the rich dark soil of potential. I see it in the faces of my children, the hopes of my friends, and the vision of my peers. When they come to me, they aren't looking for empty, gratuitous words or idle observations. They need my help laying out boundaries and perimeters inside which they are free to construct their dreams. They need curbs—reliable curbs. Curbs that show them where it's safe to build.

Boundaries liberate the contractor in all of us, assuring consistent support through the ebb and flow of life. Yesterday, an open field; tomorrow, a neighborhood. Yesterday, a dream; tomorrow, a life fulfilled.

Have a great week.

Marv's

As we pulled together final details for Mary's parents' fiftieth wedding anniversary, my wife gave me specific directions and placed the checkbook in my hand. My chore, she explained, was to retrieve two sheet cakes from a store called Marv's.

Marv's has been a part of Brighton, Michigan, for years. At one point it sat on the outside edge of town, but over time, town has grown right into Marv's neighborhood. My fifteen-minute journey took me past many properties that have been built within the past five years, including super-stores, mega-stores, wholesale stores, and membership-only stores. These national chains all have attractive new facilities and exceptionally competitive prices. The location for each store was carefully selected and laid out in compliance with demographic studies. They were great stores, but I was headed for Marv's.

Finally on my right, I saw a dated neon sign with an even more dated frame structure behind it. The parking lot was laid out poorly and there were precious few open spots. I finally saw a car backing out of a narrow opening and slipped my van into it. As I pushed through the front door, I was immediately taken back by what I found. To my right, there was a complete butcher counter, to my left, a well-stocked bakery counter and display. A sizable crowd stood in front of both.

The customers were primarily local folks, who knew Marv's. Many of the employees wore flour-dusted and frosting-stained aprons that showed they had personally made most of the items in the counters that separated us. They really knew what they were talking about. Several hours later, when I took a bite of the chocolate-covered cherry masterpiece I had purchased, I understood why a crowd was willing to search for a parking spot and wait patiently in line. There was nothing mega, super, or wholesale about Marv's. Just frosting-stained excellence.

Marv didn't study consumer demographics or population patterns. He didn't care much for convenience, but he did and still does do something better than anybody else in Brighton. That reputation keeps his parking lot full and his customers satisfied and loyal.

In a mega, super, wholesale world, I want to do what Marv did. I want to be worth the inconvenience. Worth the extra miles. Worth the wait. I want my contribution to be unique. My effort personal. I want to be known as the best in town—just like Marv's!

Have a great week.

Merge Generously

My typical route to work requires me to take a sweeping left turn from Seventy-fifth Street to Interstate Thirty-five. The volume of travelers that follow the same route necessitates a two-lane turn. The result is that on the short ramp that leads to the high-speed expressway, a good deal of merging has to take place.

I've noticed that most people employ one of two approaches when making their move into a single entrance line. They either press to the furthest point possible, unconcerned about cutting off another driver, or they lie back, content to wait their turn. I must confess that when I started taking this route, I did my very best to get the nose of my vehicle as far forward as I possibly could. That was until it occured to me that the extra twenty to thirty feet are generally not worth the hassle. Now, I am content to lie back and merge at a more natural pace.

Interestingly, I've noticed that when I tap my brakes and hang back, there is rarely an acknowledgment from the driver of the car I've allowed to move into place in front of me. When I was more aggressive in my driving style, I attributed my enhanced position in line to my outstanding ingenuity and skill. I didn't need to thank anyone because I'd made my own way, carved my own path. Now I realize how wrong I was. And it's made me think about something else: the people who have selflessly made room for me throughout my life.

I can now put names next to the brake lights that have been illuminated on my behalf—family, friends, managers, and co-workers. They've slowed their own progress for a time, in order to create a place for me. And they've done so without recognition or reward.

There are many places in life where two lanes become one, at least for a time. If order is to triumph over chaos, then someone has to be willing to tap the brakes. If you've made a place for me, thanks. If I have ignorantly and arrogantly pushed on without acknowledging your act of kindness, I'm sorry.

Merge wisely. Merge graciously. Merge generously.

Have a great week.

Wakes

On final approach into Kansas City International Airport last Friday night, I caught a glimpse of a local lake that was teeming with people engaged in water sports. The ninety-plus temperatures and high humidity have pushed this sort of activity to the top of the priority heap for many able-bodied individuals.

As I watched, I began to notice a distinct pattern that helped to identify the various water vehicles. In addition to the traditional speedboats that would typically populate a summertime lake, there were a large number of small, jet-powered wave runners and jet-skis. The picture made me remember a recent conversation with a friend. He had mentioned that more and more water skiers are changing to the newer jet-powered marine vessels because they leave no wake behind them. With the bird's eye view I was enjoying, I could validate his point.

Behind each speedboat, there was a noticeable wake that fanned out from the back of the boat with ever increasing width as it distanced itself from the origin. This wake opened up against the naturally formed waves in defiance of the flow. On the other hand, wave runners had no comparable impact. Instead, as they buzzed around with incredible agility and speed, they left very little in the way of a lasting impression on their environment.

As the wheels of the DC9 hit the runway, I couldn't help but wonder: *Do I leave a wake as I move through life? Do I impact my environment? Do I make a lasting impression? Is the impression I make strong enough to resist the flow of the status quo?*

A premium has been placed on living a wakeless life. Individualism and autonomy with limited accountability are far more the norm today. It can be unpopular to take a stand or carve a path. It takes courage, wisdom, and strength of character.

I'm thankful for those who have courageously cut a path in front of me. Their wake has helped to keep me on course more times than I know. I want to be that same kind of person—someone who makes a difference. Someone who creates a wave with enough force to challenge conventional thinking and pessimism. I want to generate waves that continue to hit the shore long after I am gone.

Have a great week.

21

Listen to the Music

Greetings to you
this Monday morning.

As the two teams began to warm up for the pending basketball game, members of the pep band began filling a small reserved section immediately across from us. The band was comprised of students with instruments that ranged from a snare drum to a violin. I've always enjoyed the added dimension that a band brings to a ball game, and I anticipated the music that was to come.

It wasn't long before all of the members of the group were seated and prepared. With the wave of the conductor's baton, they began to play. To my surprise and disappointment, the performance was awful. There was very little coordination, little consistent rhythm, and in general, very little entertainment value. As I listened, I noticed that many of the songs played, although masked in inexperience, were familiar pieces. Some were classic marches; others were more contemporary compositions. In many cases, as

I listened to the rendition of the work, my mind played the well-known version with which I was familiar—powerful, effective, and filled with grace. No doubt the same version that the band members and their instructor knew. The version that had compelled them to attempt the work in the first place.

In the weeks since this experience, I have spent time with several people who I greatly respect. I have listened to a number of tunes being played. The music ranged from parenting to strategic thinking—from family service and support to financial planning, and in many cases, they were being performed better than my version of the same piece.

Over and over I was transported to that rural Kansas gymnasium and the telling comparison between performance and design. Over and over I realized, with humility, that I have much to learn from others who play their music with more power, effectiveness, and grace.

Never stop listening to those who play the music better than you do. Instead, learn from them and let them have an impact upon the way you play. Let it change your methods, your rhythm, and your practice habits for the better. It will help you play each piece as it was intended in all the concerts of your life.

Have a great week.

Shims

The latest activity associated with the renovation of my basement centers around the installation and trimming out of windows and doors. Both of these activities are time consuming and expensive. As a result, I took an hour-long class at a local home supply store to make certain I was informationally equipped to tackle the assignment.

Early in the course, the instructor let us know that getting things "square" was a vital part of getting them to work properly. He then pulled out a ninety-nine-cent pack of shims and went to each critical location of the work, showing how an appropriately placed sliver of wood can be used to "true up" a job. There he was, surrounded by a store full of expensive materials and tools, yet the single item he needed to square it all up was well . . . an unassuming pack of shims worth less than a buck.

Shims are small wedge-shaped pieces of wood that can be used individually or in a stack to adjust the height or width of a completed piece of work. Carefully adding these shims allows subtle but significant changes to be made, ensuring that the finished product is level, true, accurate, and effective. Shims aren't seen. They are inserted, tacked in place and then covered up. Yet without them, the value and beauty of the work is greatly diminished.

I am aware of a number of humble and caring people who act as shims in my life. They see my low spots and endeavor to adjust them. These wonderful people are willing to stay behind the scenes, playing this critical role for me. They know that I often resist, convinced that my work is level without them. But they know better. They know that without the subtle yet significant adjustments they bring to my life, the picture would be forever tilted.

A listening ear, a knowing look, a wise word, a gentle nudge, a bold confrontation; whatever form it takes, I am thankful for what these people do to "true up" the door posts and window frames of my life.

Have a great week.

Don't Miss the Walk

Just outside our back door we have a basket that contains a black retractable leash, along with other odds and ends. The leash does what leashes are suppose to do. It confines, constrains, and controls Mackie, our ten-year-old mutt. Given the restrictive nature of this device, you would assume that Mackie would resent it. In reality, the opposite is true.

Her willingness to accept the leash has nothing to do with the fact that it is designed to protect her and others but rather that it is associated with an enjoyable activity— going for a walk. When Mackie sees me retrieve the leash from the basket, she is instantly transformed into a happy puppy. She dances and jumps in complete delight because she knows we're going for an adventure.

Forget the confinement, set aside the fact that there is control involved, the knowledge that the leash is linked to an activity as wonderful as a walk far outweighs any negative aspects. In a sense it is the control that brings freedom. In our town a dog without a leash isn't free to walk. Quite literally, the leash provides control and freedom at the same time. She may tug against it, but instinctively she knows it is the only way that a walk will happen.

Control has become an unpopular concept these days. Rules are passé. Restrictions are a matter of personal convenience. Yet when painted on the canvas of opportunity, control can open up a multi-colored world. A seatbelt on an airplane restricts and controls your movements, but once you are safely strapped in, the world expands at five hundred miles an hour. A stop light at a busy intersection is designed to control and restrain your movement, but it is the only way to avoid chaos and collision.

The leashes in my life aren't handheld or retractable, but I'm glad they are there. For inside their confines, I discover the freedom I need to enjoy the adventure of life. Without a leash, I would miss the walk.

Have a great week.

That's Hal's Job

Last week David Cone made a return visit to Kansas City, now as a member of the New York Yankees. His return reminded me of a lesson I had learned from him while he was playing for the Kansas City Royals.

My family and I attended a game that proved to be a great pitcher's duel. Both warriors had made it to the ninth inning, with only one run separating the two teams. David Cone climbed the mound for the Royals, needing only three outs. He was throwing his warm-up pitches when the manager emerged from the dugout. When Hal McRae made the motion to the bullpen to bring in a relief pitcher, the crowd erupted in boos. It seemed obvious to us that David Cone deserved a chance to finish his own game. Instead, the outcome was being taken out of his hands and committed to an individual who had recently blown a similar opportunity.

The big-screen TV in left field showed Cone in the dugout, shaking hands with teammates, grinning with satisfaction at the job he had done. There was no disgust in his look, no apparent objection to being pulled. I speculated out loud that it must have been his decision to sit out the ninth, but I was wrong.

In a post-game interview, David Cone talked about his willingness to go the ninth. He felt physically and mentally up to the task. But, as he so clearly put it, that was not his call to make. The responsibility for that decision rested squarely with the manager, and no one else. Hal's job is not seeing to it that David Cone goes a full nine innings. Hal's job is to take the raw material he's been given and form it into a winner. Not for one game or two, but for one hundred sixty-two games. David Cone understood that. He knew that his job was to pitch until instructed otherwise, not to second guess leadership decisions. He understood that a tremendous individual performance only works inside the context of team commitment.

Do your best. Throw every pitch with all the precision and velocity you can muster. Throw strikes. Then remember that pitching the ninth might not be your job. The season is long; wise mangers understand that, and team players support it.

Have a great week.

Polyurethane

Greetings to you
this Monday morning.

This past weekend I spent many hours working with polyurethane. I had doors and trim to coat with the milky white substance in an effort to check one more item off my list of home fix-up tasks. I got significantly more than I bargained for in the process.

I expected a time-consuming and slow-moving assignment, and indeed that was what I got. I expected the preparation work, the mess, the clean up, and the smell, again without disappointment. I even accurately anticipated the hours involved. What I underestimated was how much I would actually enjoy what I was doing. As I applied the clear coat, the hidden beauty of the wood seemed to come alive.

The wood that I had picked off the shelf at my local home improvement store, the wood that I had measured, mitered, stained, and nailed, the very same wood that on occasion had left splinters in my hands, now glowed with an unanticipated beauty that far exceeded my expectations.

Later in the day when Mary toured the work site, she immediately commented on how nice the doors looked. The grain seemed to come alive with distinctive patterns and color. She made no mention of the polyurethane. The task that had taken me hours to perform was never referenced.

The entire experience has made me a real fan of polyurethane. It's a humble product. A product with the sole objective of making anything it touches more pronounced, more obvious, more beautiful. It doesn't expect or receive accolades, but delights in exposing the grain in other objects. It's transparent and tough, clinging ruthlessly to whatever it is applied.

Those wonderful characteristics illustrate what I would like to be. Instead, I am more like a coat of paint. Full coverage, single color, highly identifiable, leaving my mark wherever I go. What if instead I embraced the role of making everyone I touch more beautiful? Clearer? More unique? I don't want to change you. I want to bring out the beauty in you. Your beauty. Your grain. Your uniqueness. What if. . . .

Have a great week.

Translating Danish

Greetings to you
this Monday morning.

A t the conclusion of a successful day of meetings in our London office, a business colleague and I looked for an appropriate place to hook our laptop computers into the corporate network. It was now early evening. We had been isolated all day, and we needed to review our growing electronic mail inboxes. We also had to follow up on several items that had come to light in the course of our daily meetings.

I hooked my machine into the network and began the arduous task of sifting through my e-mail. But my colleague, Claus, took a different path. After setting up his laptop on the desk, he placed a telephone call. I quickly determined that his call was to his home. His family, which includes his wife and three small children, live in Copenhagen.

In just a few minutes, Claus was immersed in full, joyous conversation. From time to time, I could hear the lighthearted, youthful tones generated from the other end of the line. The expressiveness of the voices in Copenhagen was unmistakable, as was the inflection of the words. Claus listened intently as story after story was shared. From time to time, the voice changed in Denmark as another one of the Pedersens took the lead.

Claus communicated thoughtfully and attentively with his family. He listened and loved, all remotely. The children were most certainly speaking with the same individual with whom I'd just spent the day interacting, but to them his identity was wrapped up in one simple word: Daddy. Their love for him and their desire for him to share their daily experiences was obvious, as was his delight in being called to such a task.

Although I couldn't translate one word exchanged, I understood perfectly. Language is no obstacle for true communication. Joy, delight, and love burst through with perfect clarity. In those waning moments of the day, I heard them say, "You're important to me." "I want you to know all about my day" and "I love you." All without knowing a single word of Danish. Isn't honest communication wonderful?

Have a great week.

Shifting Sands

Several years ago my family and I explored the South Forelands Lighthouse along the breathtaking bluffs close to Dover, England. The construction of the tower was necessitated by a phenomenon known as the Goodwin Sands. Three miles offshore this imposing sandbar extends along the English Channel at a width of three miles and a length of ten miles. Sailors dubbed it "The Swallowing Sands," as over time it claimed many vessels and the crews on board. What made the sands especially imposing was their dynamic nature. Shifting, unpredictable, and unforgiving, they made sea travel dangerous from St. Margaret's Bay to Thanet.

Seasoned sailors know all of the lighthouses along the English coast by the distinct light patterns that they produce. The South Forelands Lighthouse is uniquely identified by its three flashes within a twenty-second time period. A beautifully designed Victorian turntable and a clockwork mechanism make this possible. The powerful light turns with perfection as it pulsates its distinct warning. Once the unmistakable beam has been conveyed, safety is then in the hands of the ship's captain. The South Forelands Lighthouse has done its job.

Predictable, reliable, and distinct; these are qualities that convert a monument into a friend. I need lighthouses, reference points, traveling companions, and warning beacons in my life. Individuals who uniquely signal the danger in the shifting sand. Friends who won't captain my ship, but whose light faithfully penetrates the fog and darkness of my uncertainty.

I, too, am a lighthouse. The older I get, the fewer ships I actually captain. My time and energy are more often used to influence, advise, warn, and illuminate the way for others. Throughout the journey, my charge is loyalty, honor, and courage to stand as a true and trustworthy companion in the face of the storm.

The sand shifts and because it does there are many opportunities to run aground or lose your way. Watch for the lighthouses along the shore. Take full advantage of the messages they pulsate. Then pound out your warning to those who look your way.

Have a great week.

Battle On!

Several years ago, on a Saturday afternoon amid the grand fall colors, the unblocked sunshine, and the cool breezes, my family and I watched as a group of pilots reenacted the incredible attack on Pearl Harbor. What we witnessed was something that I think we will all remember for a long time to come. World War II vintage planes, painted with great detail to capture the look of the Japanese bombers, poured over a reconstructed U.S. Base.

To add an even greater sense of realism, explosive devices were detonated on the ground. Over and over the planes circled and swooped down through the plumes of smoke, simulating an attack, then pulling up to begin the assault process again. While this outstanding effort was merely a small illustration of the events that actually took place on that cool December morning in 1942, it did serve as a potent lesson on the history of our country.

Today, this devastating defeat for the United States military is a chapter in our history books. It is awesome and terrifying, but it could have been much more. It could have meant the end of our nation's power and influence in the world. But instead, great resolve rose from the ashes of defeat. That resolve bred commitment, and commitment perseverance, and perseverance brought victory.

Margaret Thatcher once said: "You may have to fight a battle more than once to win it." That's perseverance. It's standing firm against whatever seems to be pounding the shores of your life that would force you to give in or give up. It's pressing on when the black smoke of defeat seems to surround you.

Most of us will never have to face a battle like the one my family and I saw reenacted last Saturday. Yet every one of us has been and will continue to be faced with the relentless pressure to give up on much of what we value. Our families, our beliefs, our dreams, and our integrity stand in the balance. May we find hope through the ashes, courage in the defeats, and humility in the victories. Battle on. It is worth the fight.

Have a great week.

The Shutter Clicks

I love to snow ski. The exhilaration, the speed, the refreshment all add up to a wonderful recreational experience. This year, I enjoyed a vacation with my family at one of the most beautiful locations we've ever visited. We had heard wonderful things about the Canadian Rockies. So we made our way to an area just outside of Calgary, Alberta. On two of the days, we skied in weather that was absolutely perfect with an unrestricted view of the breathtaking scenery.

Each run down the mountain took concentration, focus, and energy. On one such run, with my attention fully channeled toward the task at hand, the pristine quiet was broken by the sound of a camera shutter. I glanced up long enough to see a young couple having their picture taken with one of the awesome mountain panoramas as a backdrop. In the seconds immediately following, I realized that I had inadvertently skied behind the pair just as the photograph was being snapped. Along with gleeful smiles, crisp white snow, and monumental peaks, they had also captured the image of a stranger from Kansas—someone they'll never see again. A person without a name had left a permanent record on their moment in time.

Life affords us the opportunity to gather around those we know and love in a fully orchestrated pose. Often we are deeply connected to companion images with whom we share the frame. However, life is spontaneous. Candid. It propels us into the snapshots of others. Those we may only connect with once. A waiter in a restaurant. The guy from Kalamazoo sitting in the next seat on an airplane. A child in the grocery store.

Don't be fooled. A single moment in time can project a permanent record. One moment, one brief exchange, one fleeting flash, one lasting image. The next time you step or ski into someone else's snapshot, make the most of the opportunity. The experience may not last more than a few seconds, but the image could end up in an album for life.

The shutter clicks hundreds of times each day, and very few of those shots are planned.

Have a great week.

European Shaves

Not long ago, I realized that I was getting much closer shaves in Europe than in the United States. Yes, I said *shaves!* At first, I discounted this phenomenon, but over time, I have begun to understand why my initial impressions were correct.

When I travel in Europe, I always use an electric shaver. Even though I use the same shaver at home, I don't get the same results. Over time, I have identified two factors that I believe contribute to this increased performance during my European trips. First, in Europe, the power source runs at 220 volts, but only 110 volts run through the outlet in my bathroom at home. It's obvious from the sound that the shaver blades move at a significantly faster rate when my shaver has been charged at the higher voltage.

Second, nearly every hotel at which I have stayed in Europe has a small circular mirror located by the bathroom sink. This mirror provides a magnified view of the area being shaved. Stubble that would escape my non-corrected morning vision is plainly visible, allowing me to concentrate my attention and energy in the right direction.

Last week at the office, my enlightened views on shaving came to mind as I was sifting through a stack of work on my desk. I was having difficulty focusing on one task because there were so many others clouding my vision. Even when I attempted to wrap something up, I often left behind the stubble of the nearly complete. Additionally, I often view these tasks as solo assignments, a factor that limits the power that I can allocate to the work involved. As with my shaving, the problem rested somewhere between a distracted view and a diluted power source.

Sometimes I need a magnified view of the problems I'm facing before I can conquer them. At other times I need more power—the increased voltage I get by involving others in the challenges that life throws my way.

Enhance your view of the challenges that you face. Get some focus. Then find the power to help you deal with what you've just discovered. Power without focus is dangerous. Clear vision without power brings a sense of hopelessness. Power and focus together yield dramatic results.

Have a great week.

Hair Cuts

Several weeks ago a friend of mine approached me with a question. He had a young son and wanted to know if there were any words of advice I could share with him—a secret or two from a father whose sons weren't so young any more. The question caught me off guard, and the pat answer I gave him disappointed both of us. It wasn't until later that an important insight hit me.

I got to thinking about my college days and a lesson I learned that was born out of sheer financial desperation. I needed cash so I learned to cut hair. I don't actually recall who I learned on, but my friends were carefree and willing to give me a chance. In return, I was willing to adjust my rates. When I graduated from college in 1977, I not only had a degree but a loosely defined skill as well.

This skill didn't come into play again until it was time to trim my son Andrew's fine baby locks. Mary trusted me with a pair of sharp scissors even next to her son's tiny ears. The experience brought a new dimension to our father/son relationship.

Andrew is no longer a baby. In fact, he is almost eigteen. My younger son Erik is sixteen, and between them they've each had two haircuts that I didn't personally provide. That means that during the past eighteen years, I've given more than 275 haircuts. If I assume that an average cut takes me thirty minutes, then I've spent more than 137 hours literally within inches of my two boys. We talk, laugh, listen, encourage, and even cut a little hair.

Piles of hair clippings and hundreds of precious conversations have resulted. These haircuts have taken place in the basement, the garage, out on the deck, in the driveway, and in the bathroom. But regardless of the location, they have always been one-on-one, father-to-son, friend-to-friend communications—some of the best and most honest moments we have had.

My advice to that young father would be different now. I would encourage him to buy a sharp pair of scissors, a durable clipper, and prepare to meet his son for thirty uninterrupted minutes every six weeks. What begins as a financial necessity can become a relational gold mine. Make the investment.

Have a great week.

More Than Vapor

Last Thursday was one of those days when the weather seems absolutely perfect—not a cloud in the sky. I was returning to my office building after lunch when I looked up and noticed a vapor trail in the sky—this was not a jet but rather the work of a skywriter.

I stood for a few moments and admired the precision with which the first two letters were being written, and then went up to my office. Roughly thirty minutes later, I was pulled into a meeting that afforded me a perfect view of the sky where the aerial scripting had been taking place. It was quite evident that significantly more had been written, but equally as obvious that the gentle summer breezes were rapidly erasing the message from the sky. The task that had taken such skill to produce was now indistinguishable, an abstract image on a pristine blue canvas. No lasting impact, no enduring message.

Over the past month, I have had the opportunity to perform more job interviews than at any other time in my career. From recent college grads, to seasoned professionals, I've seen them all. In each case, I've received a recent copy of a resume, listing the educational and professional background and accomplishments of each. In nearly all of the interviews I have performed, I have concluded the time of interaction with a simple question, "What factors have helped shape you into the person you are today?"

Nearly every answer has been meaningful and insightful. From parents, to teachers, to grandparents, to previous managers, to books read, the answers were diverse, but always well thought out and sensitively communicated. Discovering what made indelible marks in the lives of individuals provided a vivid picture of lasting value.

Daily, scripts are written on the canvas of our life experience and in most cases, the gentle breezes of time blow them away. Yet there are those times, those people, those experiences that permanently mark our lives, and as a result, become the answer to an interview question from a perfect stranger.

Blue sky or storm, gentle breeze or gale-force wind, write messages that last. Messages not easily forgotten. Messages that inspire, encourage, motivate, and endure.

Have a great week.

Say "No" To Clouds

The longer we sat on the Munich runway, the more I doubted the likelihood of our departure. We'd been delayed at the gate for about an hour and a half because of fog, and from my vantage point, conditions hadn't improved. However, we had been instructed to board the aircraft and prepare for departure. Once away from the gate, the exterior of the Boeing jet was sprayed with a de-icing solution. By then, the thick fog had become a driving snow, coating the runway with a thin wintry coat.

I must admit, I was surprised when the captain made the announcement that we had been cleared for takeoff. I tried to imagine what it would be like for the pilot to aim the aircraft down a runway he could barely see. In the moments before lift-off, the conditions seemed to worsen, and the passengers cloaked their anxiety in an unnatural silence.

Once the rear wheels of the aircraft were off the ground, it was a matter of seconds before the ground was invisible. An instant later, light burst through the window to my left—not an artificial or muted light, but brilliant morning sunlight. It had taken only a couple of seconds for us to lose sight of the bitter conditions below, break through the clouds, and burst into the sunshine.

As I soaked up the view, I was struck by the way my perspective had changed. Sitting on the ground in my window seat, I had been convinced that the storm around me was nearly impenetrable. But just a few moments later, I had a breathtaking view of the Alps—unobscured and beautiful, while below us hung a thin, flat layer of clouds. The experience set my mind in motion.

When problems and challenges envelop me, I see only the driving snow and the oppressive fog. In the midst of the storm, I convince myself that the layer of blackness is thick and formidable. I'm tempted to turn around and return to the gate, realizing too late that my problem is nothing more than a thin, flat layer of clouds, fully obscuring the brilliance of a new opportunity. Say no to the clouds. Say yes to the promise of the morning.

Have a great week.

First Things First

This past weekend I tackled one of those easy-to-ignore jobs around the house. Although I daily use and travel through our garage, it is easy to overlook the things that beg for attention. Lawn tools in need of winter storage, bikes that need to be less conspicuously placed, paint supplies that never made it all the way back, and a host of other easy-to-misplace items created a clutter that was more than I could stand. Saturday it was time for action.

As I began the task of moving everything from the garage to the driveway, I stumbled across a purchase I had made several months earlier in response to a credit card offer which accompanied my monthly bill. The advertisement called it an "emergency car kit," designed to hold nearly every necessary tool in a case compact enough to fit under a car seat. I couldn't resist. And I was happy with my purchase until I discovered that once a few of the tools had been used and returned to the kit, it was impossible to close the case.

Saturday I rediscovered my $19.95 headache, and opened the case to take a good look at the tools inside. To my surprise, I found that the case had been constructed with a molded indentation for each item. Soon the tools were back in their places, and much to my delight, the case closed neatly and easily.

Last week, a friend asked me how I was doing. The only honest response I knew to give was "busy." The swarm, pace, and volume of life seemed overwhelming. I was doing my best to cram everything I could into my schedule, but I was beginning to sense the clutter. Then my newly appreciated $19.95 headache inspired a solution. Slow down long enough to put things back where they belong. First things first; second things second. Each in its own place. No more squeezing the case to try and get it to close. No more ignoring the mess. But rather, sorting through relationships, commitments, tasks, and responsibilities, putting each thing back where it belongs.

Having trouble getting your case closed? Take time to sort through the clutter in your life and put things where they belong. It's the only way to make it all fit, and it's called getting your priorities straight.

Have a great week.

Home Keys

Last week in the rush to get several projects moved off my "to do" list, I found myself pouring over the keys on my laptop computer. On one particular occasion, I had a significant amount of typing to finish, so I lined my notes up on the right side of my keyboard and focused my eyes fully in that direction. Having convinced myself that I was making real progress, I took a quick glance toward the screen and much to my surprise and disappointment, saw nothing more than a wild and meaningless array of letters.

Closer inspection revealed the reason for the gibberish. In the course of my typing, with attention shifted away from the keys on my keyboard, my fingers had slipped off the "home keys" and moved one letter to the right. The message I had intended to deliver, the ideas and concepts I had planned to communicate, were entirely lost.

A few days later, Mary and I traveled to Banff, Alberta, to celebrate my parent's sixtieth wedding anniversary. My father and mother had arranged a wonderful retreat for my five siblings, our spouses, and themselves. On Friday afternoon, the fourteen of us loaded into two tightly packed vans at the Calgary airport for the ninety-minute drive into the Canadian Rockies. We'd come from California, Tennessee, Illinois, and Kansas—all with one purpose: to celebrate the joy of family and the value of commitment. We also planned on having some fun along the way.

In the course of four days with my wife, parents, and siblings, I experienced something I hadn't fully anticipated. I found my home keys. Pace, schedules, deadlines, and critical demands had allowed my fingers to drift from my point of reference. Through the example and encouragement of those who love and care for me, I saw areas in my life that were beginning to turn to gibberish.

The messages I want to deliver will never get written if I can't keep my focus, my direction, my perspective, my fingers on the home keys. Before you type another word, make sure you have your focus firmly on the things that matter most.

Have a great week.

Junk Mail

I was sifting through the mail at my office one day when I came across an envelope that looked like it might contain a check. I opened it and found what did indeed look like a check for $42,800, printed on the top third of a letter-sized document.

Since I had been receiving similar promotional mailings for almost a year, I knew that this "check-like" document was not actually a check at all but an enticement to borrow money against the equity in my house for a wide variety of exciting uses. What made this particular pitch unique was the verbiage at the top.

It addressed me by name and then said, "We've valued your property at 5200 Metcalf and determined that you are qualified to borrow up to $42,800." I found this statement particularly amusing since the property at 5200 Metcalf does not belong to me. In fact, it belongs to my employer and is worth far more than the proposed $42,800 equity loan. Literally millions more. The statement had been worded to give the impression that the sender had made an individualized assessment of the property. Instead the error, which would be obvious to anyone who had even the slightest knowledge about the property, identified this document as a piece of junk mail in which the sender had invested nothing in the way of time or research.

Before I had finished laughing about the mistake, I began thinking about several conversations in which I had participated recently. Conversations with my kids related to some of the decisions they are facing. Conversations with staff members about their families. Conversations with Mary about the new year and the goals we have. Conversations that on the surface would indicate that I place great value on these people. Conversations that will reveal the extent of my research.

It's easy to give the impression that you value those around you. We pretend to know their worth. Yet we make offers that understate and diminish the equity of the individual.

Don't send junk messages. Prove to those around you that you understand their true value. A value that time and involvement fully exposes.

Have a great week.

True Fans

Just before the 1998 baseball season concluded in Kansas City, my twelve-year-old daughter and I decided to take in a game. We were able to get great seats, which quite frankly wasn't difficult given that the Royals were playing the Detroit Tigers. Both teams were well out of contention for any post-season play, and the crowd filled less than 25 percent of the stadium.

With the game having little impact on the current season, the managers saw fit to use players that they had just recruited from their minor league operations, giving these players opportunity to show their prowess at the big-league level. One of the players that the Tigers fielded on the brisk pre-fall evening was a catcher by the name of Rob Fick. Under most circumstances, a player like Fick would have gone unnoticed, but three men seated near us made that impossible. Any time Fick made a professional-caliber play, these three men would cheer with unusual enthusiasm.

In the middle of the game, with one Tiger already on base, Rob Fick hit his first major-league home run. He showed no emotion as he rounded the bases, but the three men situated behind us were absolutely beside themselves, celebrating with high fives, hoots, cheers, and spontaneous laughter.

An inning later I could stand the suspense no more. I worked my way down to where the three men were seated and engaged them in conversation. Rob Fick's initiation into the majors was shared by two brothers and a close friend who had flown in from California for the occasion. A largely empty stadium, a disinterested crowd, and a meaningless outcome were no damper for them. They were there to cheer for one person. Their brother and friend had made it, and with a home run as an exclamation point, they had something to celebrate.

Cheer for each other. Delight in the accomplishments of others. Celebrate home runs you didn't hit, especially when it seems that the rest of the audience wasn't watching. Show the people you care about that you're their biggest fan. Erase all doubt in the minds of those you love. Cheer for them.

Have a great week.

Coded for Love

The past several weeks have been some of the busiest I have ever experienced in my professional life. I have been pulled many different directions in an attempt to keep systems operational, clients connected, hardware humming, and plans on schedule. As a result, I've spent very little time actually in my office. My trusty pager notifies me that somewhere out there someone needs to speak with me, and the seven-digit number displayed on the little device that clips on my belt indicates who that person is.

For Mary and me, having a pager fills another important need. It serves as a link for the kids when we go out for the evening. Knowing that we are only a page away in case of some unforeseen circumstance puts our minds at rest. At first we assumed it would be used only in emergencies, but we have found that it is helpful to confirm that a certain task has been completed in our absence through a series of pager codes we developed.

For instance, "when you get Alli tucked in bed, page us and let us know that everything went as planned." For this task, we chose the numbers 04, as a representation for OK. This code has served its purpose beautifully. Then we added 143, which simply means I love you. Added to the 143 was the trailing number that represents the age of the sender, thus indicating who has originated the page. When Mary and I are out running an errand, shopping, or on a much-needed date, we receive the welcome 1439 or 14312 or 14314, indicating that everyone is headed off to bed.

Last week this system took on even more meaning and value. In the midst of all the pages from those individuals who needed business related support from me, I started getting periodic pager reminders from home. There in four or five digits, in an area normally reserved for telephone numbers, I was sent a burst of encouragement that seemed to boost my spirits like nothing else could have. A 143 in the midst of the chaos.

Next time you think it's hard to communicate your love to someone, just remember 143. I'm so grateful that four people in my life did.

By the way family, 14340.

Have a great week.

The Wrong Jam

One of my favorite radio stations operates with a news format and originates in Chicago. Given my roots in the city and my affinity for the local Chicago sports teams, I like to tune in whenever I can.

On my way home one evening last week, while my radio was tuned to my station of choice, I became preoccupied with my effort to navigate through the rush of Kansas City traffic. For several moments, I was oblivious to the chatter on the air waves, until the topic switched to a full-scale rush-hour traffic report. Words like *hold-ups, construction, accident, detours,* and *delays,* quickly snapped my attention back to the radio. I listened dutifully for several seconds, hoping to obtain some useful information, until the obvious struck me. As much as I enjoy the Chicago news station, information pertaining to the traffic challenges in the Chicago area are of no value to me as I fight my way through Kansas City traffic.

I certainly empathized with all those who were hung up on the Kennedy, Dan Ryan, Edens, and Eisenhower Expressways, but their plight had nothing to do with the challenges I was facing. I felt badly for the people in the Windy City whose dinners would have to be warmed in a microwave, but their dilemma had no impact on the meal being prepared for me in suburban Kansas.

On any given day, we receive more information than we can possibly use. Consequently, we're left sorting out what applies to us from what does not. Our filtering systems are stretched to the max. There are plenty of useful facts, but many more that simply don't match the questions we have. When I'm stuck in traffic in Kansas, I don't need Illinois answers. I need to tune into the answers that apply to me.

That's a good rule to follow before you give or take advice. Make sure that the question is understood well before a solution is offered. The helicopter circling over the loop in Chicago can't see the jam I'm in. Filter the facts and make sure they apply to your neighborhood before you change your course.

Have a great week.

Leading
from Behind

This past weekend, duty required me to carry a number of items from the driveway, around the house, to the basement door in the back. Because our house sits on a lot that falls off rapidly from front to back, the journey down is substantially easier than the trip back up.

To accompany me on these trips back and forth, I enlisted the services of Mackie, our nine-year-old mutt. Although Mackie doesn't have quite the same puppy spirit that she had a few years ago, she still seems overjoyed to have my companionship and attention. Each time I began to make my way from our basement door back up to the driveway, I would spur her on to beat me to the top. Each time, she would heed the call, pass me, and race energetically up the hill.

At the top, she would disappear around the front corner of the house, then quickly circle around a tree and peak back down the hill at me. Her reason for doing so was simple. She wanted to make sure that I was still behind her. She needed our eyes to connect, and approval to be given with a fleeting glance. She just needed assurance that while she was running on ahead, conquering the hill, I was still there, noting her triumph.

This Saturday morning exercise reminded me of a leadership principle I often overlook—sometimes leadership is more about following than leading. Sometimes leadership means encouraging others to burst to the front, to show the way, to beat a path. Sometimes leadership is about catching the eyes of those we've spurred on and assuring them that we're still cheering them on, still encouraging them to stay the course. A good leader does not always have to be out in front, leading the pack.

A true leader celebrates with others. He or she points the way, gives the charge, then openly delights in the victory. A true leader commits to be there in the midst of the journey, encouraging, condoning, and watching—a few steps back, a bit more winded, but there, within reach, and on the same path.

Point the way, follow on, then celebrate. You'll be amazed at how much leading can be done without having to be out front.

Have a great week.

Two-On-Two

Late Saturday afternoon, Andrew had a couple of friends over for two-on-two basketball. Andrew's plan was to use his little brother as the fourth player in this all-out, no-fouls-called competition, but Erik wasn't around. I had just finished some work around the house and was thinking about relaxing until it was time to throw some bratwurst on the grill when Andrew recruited me to round out the field.

Andrew quickly assured his friends that they need not worry, I would be on his team, and moments later we were immersed in the heat of competition. In those first few moments of play, my mind raced to the days when Andrew, Erik, and two of their friends would square off with me in a little four-on-one competition. Wow, had things ever changed. I found myself in the familiar position of being the oldest, but in addition, I was the slowest, the shortest, the heaviest, the stiffest, the most out of shape, and the most likely to embarrass himself and his seventeen-year-old son.

A few minutes into the game I began to feel more comfortable with my ability to contribute and relieved that my age had created a certain fear/respect that made the two opposing teenagers less likely to give it all they had. As the game turned into games, the competition heated up accordingly.

With four games complete, we had each registered two wins. The final and deciding game was underway. The first team to eleven baskets would win. We both neared the critical milestone at about the same rate. On one of the final possessions, I whipped a pass to Andrew who was flying full speed toward the hoop. He caught the pass, laid the ball in, and without a second thought reached out to "give me five." In that single gesture he made the hour of sweat and the subsequent days of soreness worthwhile.

Andrew's encouragement caused me to flashback to the many times I had prodded, instructed, demonstrated, and rewarded his efforts. In that instant, on that Saturday afternoon, the encourager had become the encouragee. With one simple gesture, one hand slapping another, we celebrated more than winning a game, we celebrated the changing of roles.

Invest in encouragement, and some day you'll receive it back in full.

Have a great week.

Preparing to Win

The world watched as individuals and teams from nations all over the globe took a shot at greatness. I sat in front of our television for hours, taking in the variety of events and awards ceremonies. As I watched I tried to imagine what it would be like to step up to the podium and be recognized as the best the world has to offer.

Yet, Olympic glory takes more than one great race on one isolated day in a festive town in front of a watching world. It is the result of weeks, months, even years of preparation. Olympic glory is won in weight rooms, on country roads, in private gyms, on undersized ice rinks, and on remote slopes all around the world. It's just that once every four years the world stops to pay attention. It is the final exam for a class that has required countless hours of study and many quizzes along the way.

Indiana University basketball coach, Bobby Knight has said, "The will to win is not nearly as important as the will to prepare to win."

For those of us in the mainstream of life, each day is another day of preparation, as well as another final exam. It is a workout as well as a race. We're given opportunities to hone our skills, while at the same time, we are being challenged to prove our expertise to the world. Life urges us to move on, to grow, to stretch, to learn, to build, and then to execute. It's natural to watch the world's best athletes, believing that our moment of glory and success has passed us by. We probably won't ever climb a victor's podium or wear an Olympic metal. Yet, I believe moments of challenge and opportunity greet us each new day.

We all want to be champions. The real question is whether we have the willingness and passion to prepare for the opportunities we are afforded. Gold medallists aren't made in one shining moment. Preparation is the only way to a championship. Is it worth it to you?

Have a great week.

Heights

As a junior in high school, I was given the opportunity to earn some money working for a company that painted the exterior surfaces of houses. The crews were primarily made up of college students, but as fall neared and the work force began to return to distant campuses, they looked for a few high school students to fill in the ranks. I seized the opportunity.

I knew very little about painting but convinced myself that it was something I could learn. My assumptions were correct, with one small exception—heights. After I'd had a couple of days on solid ground, I was told to climb a ladder and paint an area on the second floor of a house. I hadn't had much experience working on a ladder, let alone an expandable rib plank.

I successfully ascended the ladder and stepped out onto the plank. However, one quick glance at the ground did me in. I was frozen with fear. With a bucket of paint in one hand, and a paint brush in the other, I stood looking straight ahead, convinced that I would miss my high school graduation because I would never be able to move from that spot. Then I noticed a small nail protruding from the side of the house. The head of the nail extended about an inch and a half from the chipping paint, and I quickly wrapped the index finger of my right hand around it and hung on tightly.

Certainly logic told me that if something happened to the scaffolding, my body would have been a pile in the front yard, and my right index finger would have been left as the only remnant of a second-story painter. In reality, the plank I distrusted offered the only real stability and security.

By the summer of 1976, after five years of ladders, rib planks, and paint brushes, I'd learned what to hold on to. I knew what would give me the stability to move forward, as well as what could offer me little more than a false sense of security. Make certain that what you grasp is worth your trust.

Have a great week.

Asking for Edits

Greetings to you
this Monday morning.

This past week, a business associate brought me a copy of a document that he had been working on and asked me to read it. He was looking for input on everything from misspelled words to content. I believed that he wanted my honest feedback, so I took the time to look over what he had written, and offered my comments on it.

I scrawled my notes across the well-constructed piece of work and walked it to the author's office. One page at a time I went through the comments I had jotted down, my copy now positioned opposite the master copy. Listening intently, my coworker made notes of his own, on his document. After the brief exchange, mutual appreciation was expressed, and I returned to my office.

Since that day in my coworker's office, I've had time to reflect on this interesting exchange. My associate, and friend, had put in a great deal of hard work to produce an excellent document, yet he wanted my perspective on what he had done. He wanted another set of eyes to scrutinize what he had written. He wanted to do his best to make the end product better, and he gave me the opportunity to contribute to that cause.

Who edits your work? To whom do you take the chapters of your life story and ask for input? Is there someone you trust to point out the typos, punctuation errors, and content miscues of your story? I hope so. You might never get these issues resolved unless you are willing to risk the scrutiny of another set of eyes.

I'm thankful that I work with individuals who want what they produce to be outstanding, and I take my role in that process very seriously. I am also thankful for the healthy reminder this week of my own need for personal accountability; an editorial look at what I'm writing daily on the blank pages of my life history. While it may be difficult, even painful, at times, I'm glad there are people in my life who have the courage to raise a red pen in my direction.

Have a great week.

Listening to Your Failures

Last week, my daughter Alli brought home an assignment about inventions and inventors. At the conclusion of her work, I asked her to give me a brief summary of the various inventions that she found the most interesting. At this point in her life, her attention was captivated by such blockbuster innovations as Silly Putty™ and the Slinky™.

However, as she relayed these stories to me, a consistent theme began to emerge. It seemed that many ingenious inventions were the direct result of the failure of another endeavor. An idea that started with one particular direction in mind made a ninety-degree turn enroute to ultimate success. What started out on the drawing board looking one way, appeared in the patent office looking like something quite different.

This led me to the conclusion that inventors have developed a certain philosophy about failure and defeat. They have learned that most ideas don't go as planned and successful inventions most often rise up from the fertile ash heap on the laboratory floor. They have discovered that the designer's trashcan turns into a wellspring of thought for the tenacious mind. They have adopted the attitude that a failure is a successful idea waiting to happen.

Personally, I'm not crazy about failure. I prefer to have my ideas fly on the first attempt. But life typically doesn't work that way. Failure breeds several responses. For some, it provides ample reason to quit, for others failure fuels a more determined, "win-at-all-cost" response. It seems that inventors, on the other hand, listen to their failures as ardently as they listen to their successes. Failure may, at times, be a cruel teacher, but it will instruct nonetheless. Wise students learn from failure as well as success, and inventors build from both.

The next time you find yourself knee-deep in ashes, don't quit; don't get more bullheaded and stubborn. Sift through those ashes for new ideas, better ideas, mind-expanding ideas, ideas that work—ideas that can change the world.

Have a great week.

Plowing and Planting

Over the past weekend, I found myself traveling through several mid-western states. During my journey I got a bird's-eye view of the countless farm fields in Kansas, Missouri, and Iowa. In late April, these fields are rich black beds of anticipation. They are fertile landscapes, soaking up the spring rains in preparation for planting. Each represents the 1998 investment portfolio for the farmers that depend on them for income. A blank page, an empty canvas, an unformed lump of clay.

The deep furrows of opportunity beckon for seed, for the chance to squeeze new life out of dormant shells of potential. Last year's harvest is history. Perhaps a record year. Perhaps a bitter disappointment. The years are like that. Some more generous and abundant than dreamed possible, while others are stingy and unrelenting. They grant no guarantees and issue no condemnations. They are gone. Remembered, regretted, relished, but not revisited. Each passing year is plowed into the soil of the past.

Now is the start of a new year—to plow and to plant, to weed and to water, to agonize and anticipate, to weep and to reap.

Last week, I reached another milestone in my life. Another birthday. The same empty field of opportunity that greeted me last April greeted me again this April. I again have twelve months to grow results from dreams. To plow the good and the bad from the past, deep into the rich dark soil of hope. To make the most of the rain and sunshine, one day at a time. To set aside the worry of May's frost, July's drought, and October's flood. To give it all I've got one more time.

A new year. A field full of opportunity and hope. Dark, rich soil awaits you as well. Plow and plant.

Have a great week.

Doing What's Right

Greetings to you
this Monday morning.

My Saturday home project had me down in the basement, continuing to hammer away at my on-going remodeling effort. Therefore, I asked my fifteen-year-old son to tackle the task of mowing.

A short while later, Erik asked for my assistance in the garage. Somewhat begrudgingly I made my way up the stairs and stepped through the kitchen to the garage where I found Erik holding a container of oil. With a questioning look on his face, he asked, "Dad, is this the oil I put in the mower?" I looked at the container in his hand and recognized it as the two-cycle oil that I mix with a gallon of gas for such handy tools as the weed-whacker and leaf-blower. "No," I responded. "The oil you're looking for is over here." Without hesitation, I made my way to the plywood shelves in our garage to find the plastic bottle to which I had just referred.

As I handed Erik the bottle, I noticed a certain look in his eyes. For a few seconds, his mind seemed to be racing like the hard-drive on my computer when I've asked it to recall a large file. Then, with a hint of pain in his voice, he responded, "Dad, I've put that two-cycle oil in the mower before."

I did my best to act completely unmoved by his confession. The fact that Erik had used the wrong oil in the mower didn't concern me at all. Why would it? The mower was still running normally. The thing that caught me off guard was that Erik had in that moment of processing dealt with a dilemma. Should he or shouldn't he confess? In spite of the risk and without regard to the fact that no apparent damage had been done, Erik had opted to tell the truth. No, he did more than that; he volunteered an honest answer to a question left unasked. In short he had done what he believed was right, rather than what seemed expedient.

Not tact, not compromise, not rationalization, just a full dose of doing what's right. Should I expect less from myself?

Have a great week.

Windshield Wipers

Greetings to you
this Monday morning.

Just over a year ago, I purchased a used mini-van to serve as our primary family vehicle. So far, I've been satisfied with the decision. However, the van has exhibited one unusual characteristic—the intermittent wiper setting has a mind of its own!

I have always found this control to be useful during inclement weather in both the summer and winter months. While I've never had my windshield wiper fail to perform on demand, it does, from time to time, perform without demand. The first couple of times this happened, I wrote it off to an inadvertent touch of the wiper control. But over time, I've had to rule out that explanation. In fact, there doesn't seem to be any discernable reason for the spontaneous action of the mechanism, including weather conditions.

Without warning or provocation, the windshield wipers swing into action. Sometimes, they take one unprovoked swipe across the glass; at other times, they make four or five swings before stopping of their own accord. Sometimes it happens while I'm turning a corner; at other times, it happens while I'm driving in a straight line down a city street. Sometimes I'm sitting at a stop light; at other times, I'm cruising down an expressway. With each occurrence, the randomness seems more pronounced.

I've determined that as long as the standard performance meets my expectation, there is no need to scrutinize behavior that is above the call of duty. On the contrary, this "wiper system with a personality" has become a source of entertainment for the entire family. Regardless of where we're going or who is in the car, no matter what the mood of the moment might be, this uninvited action always invokes a lighthearted response.

Although I don't often learn lessons from car parts, my windshield wipers have taught me this: Do what's expected. Do it with precision and excellence. But every once in a while, swing into action without being asked. Be spontaneous. Wipe a windshield while the sun is shining. Exceed expectations. Provide a service that nobody has asked for or expects you to perform. Be a source of joy to someone today by doing more than is required. The reaction of the passengers will delight you.

Have a great week.

Concept Cars

This past weekend my boys and I traveled to the Kansas City International Auto Show. We've gone a few times before, and as always, we thoroughly enjoyed the experience. This year was no exception. After a visit to the show three years ago, I made the following observations, which are equally true today.

In many ways, the Auto Show is like visiting a giant showroom with every make and model of automobile you could possibly want. Yet, for me, the most interesting dimension is the opportunity to see "concept cars." In the middle of the production vehicles, next to the known and obtainable, are futurist ideas with wheels. These sleek, attention-grabbing models represent the transportation of tomorrow, and sport fascinating names like the Ford Triton™, the Plymouth BackPack™, and my favorite, the Buick Lucerne™.

I stood for awhile gazing in amazement at the Buick. When I spotted an individual to whom I could direct a question, I inquired as to when this beauty would be available. No, I didn't really think I could ever afford such a vehicle, but the possibility of seeing one gliding down the street piqued my interest. Imagine my surprise and disappointment when the response to my question was "never." The car was for show purposes only, a prototype that would provide innovations to be incorporated in production models for years to come. From sound and safety features, to climate and color, this fabulous vehicle was a sheet metal brainstorm, a test tube with a convertible top.

Then I began to wonder about my own concept cars. What ideas have I left on the drafting table because they're unobtainable? I wondered if I had been guilty of discouraging creativity in others because I measure their ideas against current reality. A sleek silver Buick™ showed me that dreams are important. Even if none of my concepts ever become reality, they may in fact spark an abundance of thought that will—thoughts that would never have been birthed had I not allowed my mind to move at concept pace.

I may never drive that beautiful automobile, but I bet that someday one of those wild features will make its way into something I will drive. I guess that's what concepts are all about. Don't be afraid to assemble one today.

Have a great week.

A Pile of Petals

A couple of weeks ago two tulips showed up in a vase on a counter by our kitchen sink. Although I'm not sure where they came from, they were a welcome bright spot in the midst of the colorlessness of winter.

Several days after they first appeared, I noticed a significant change in one of the two flowers. At the base of the vase, directly below one stem, stood a pile of petals. Not one or two petals, but every petal had been attached and ordered in a picture perfect form. The petals didn't look withered, just detached. Beside the naked stem was the fully clothed contrast.

Moments later, when Mary walked into the room, my curiosity got the better of me. Why? How? When? Her answer was amusing and telling.

Just an hour before, in the context of housework, Mary had flipped on the switch for our garbage disposal. As the unit performed in typical fashion, the characteristic vibrations radiated throughout the cabinets, counters, and everything on them. The impact on the tulips was evident.

The differences between these two flowers had been indistinguishable only hours before. They looked equally beautiful, equally strong, and equally committed to staying such. The disposal, however, revealed the truth.

For the next couple of hours the object lesson stood. Each time I glanced at it, the message resonated through my head. Although we look for and desire smooth surroundings, real life shakes. It tests our resolve. It confronts our commitment and challenges our grip. Beauty must be measured after the vibrations as well as before.

Regardless of the parallel drawn from this living analogy, the message is clear. Relationships, whether family or friends, cannot be fully measured in smooth circumstances. In the midst of life, disposals get switched on. Counters and cabinets shake, and petals fall. Problems and disappointments have a way of shaking loose anything that is not tightly bound.

The same force that exposes imposters also reveals true friends. Hold on, especially when the shaking comes.

Have a great week.

The Squeak Is Gone

For some time now I have traveled with a favorite piece of luggage. It has rolled behind me for miles through airports in the U.S. and Europe. It holds just enough clothing for a week and fits nicely into an overhead bin. Lately though, I've noticed that it sometimes gets hard to pull and develops an obnoxious squeak. It's not difficult to guess the reason why. There's a lot of friction in those moving parts, and as the wheels turn, heat is generated and grit is captured, inhibiting the wheels. The remedy is simple. Once home, I spray a little WD-40™ lubricant on the axle by both wheels, and the problem goes away, at least for a time.

Shortly after this experience, Mary and I took our first trip to Antigua in the Caribbean. This small island boasts fine beaches and an outstanding climate. As we exited from the little American Eagle™ plane onto the tarmac at the Antigua International Airport, the warm breezes greeted us like a welcoming committee. The windowless airport terminal also confirmed with resounding clarity that we weren't in Kansas any more.

When Mary first discussed the idea of taking a trip for our twentieth anniversary, the timing didn't seem right, the kids weren't covered, business pressures were building, and so many other things gave me the necessary ammunition to resist. But Mary pushed with resolve. She had noticed something in me that I had not—a squeak in my wheels and a tug that occurs when the friction is high and the load is heavy. She knew that what I needed was a blast of WD-40™, Caribbean style.

So Mary took care of the details and away we went. In actual fact I think it took a couple of days just to clear the grit out, but then as the week wore on, the wheels seemed to spin more freely. As I had expected, the work piled up while I was gone. Nearly two hundred electronic messages greeted me when I returned. However, I'm delighted to say, at least for now, the wheels are rolling smoothly again and the squeak is gone.

Have a great week.

Sense of Touch

I have spent the last two weekends wallpapering a bathroom in our home. At my side was a specially designed toolbox that holds all the various wallpapering tools I have accumulated over the years.

As I worked, I had an opportunity to use each of these valuable tools. The most valuable tool of all, however, did not come from the toolbox. At the conclusion of each section of wallpaper, I would slide my hand across the thin vinyl surface. Even when my eyes told me that the job was complete, my sense of touch told me that there were air bubbles, ripples, and other problems. My hand could feel what my eyes could not see. After all the brushing, rolling, sponging, and leveling was complete, my sense of touch provided the definitive word as to whether the paper was appropriately bonded with the wall.

Tools without touch are inadequate. Although the majority of the senses may vote in one unified block, touch knows better. That's why they don't connect a polygraph to your mouth or eyes. Touch connects. It links us physically with the object in question—no electronics, no automation, no precision instruments—just thousands of nerves evaluating and informing.

At the conclusion of the weekend, Mary prepared a lovely meal in celebration of Valentine's Day and the success of our decorating effort. We even used the dining room for the occasion. With the meal complete and the conversation in full swing, Mary reached her hand to mine. The instant that our hands touched we connected. No words were spoken, no glances exchanged. The touch was enough. Enough to say that although the job is far from done, the piece we've just completed has securely bonded— no bubbles, no ripples. Twenty-four years after our first college date, our touch told us what we needed to know.

There is no substitute. No electronic replacement. No linguistic alternative. Touch reveals more. A voice or an image can be carried thousands of miles, but a touch means you're there. Send a message. A powerful and honest message. A message that reveals the quality of your feelings. Get in touch, literally.

Have a great week.

The 645 Dog-Eared Pages

Several weeks ago, a young man named Michael approached me about speaking at his Eagle Scout ceremony. Humbled by the opportunity and unsure what I'd say, I still accepted.

As the date of the presentation approached, I did my best to prepare. To help me in the process, Michael brought his Boy Scout handbook for me to look over. As I flipped through the pages, I began to appreciate the magnitude of Michael's accomplishment—countless hours of study, difficult and demanding trips, and dozens of community projects. My initial outline on the subject of leadership began to sound pretty lame. Instead, one important question came to mind. Had all the effort been worth it?

Michael's dog-eared, 645-page workbook indicated just how substantial his investment had been. As I paged through, I saw rows and rows of assignments. Next to each were initials and a date verifying that the task had been completed. There were pictures of campsites, each accompanied by specific, detailed instructions. Notations indicated that many of these were completed in less than ideal weather conditions. It was clear that Michael had committed himself fully to becoming an Eagle Scout, the highest of the Boy Scout ranks. That commitment propelled him through the struggles along the way and helped him turn each of the 645 pages required.

As I stood to deliver my remarks, I turned to Michael who was seated behind me on the platform and asked, "Michael, was it worth it?" The sparkle in his eyes said it all. Unlike my friend Michael, I will never be an Eagle Scout. Yet his lesson to me is clear. There are investments in life that are well worth what they exact along the way. My commitment to be the best possible father, husband, manager, friend, and employee will take a lifetime to fulfill. Only then will I be able to stand and say it was worth it. Only then will I be able to celebrate the signatures on all the dog-eared pages of my life.

When you make a commitment, ask yourself the question, "Will this be worth it?" At some point, on some day, will I be able to look back and know that the reward was worth the cost?

Have a great week.

Deals on the Downside

Greetings to you this Monday morning.

S everal years ago I loaded a program on my personal computer that allows me to track household expenses. I particularly appreciate being able to balance my checkbook with ease each month. As I became comfortable with the software, I began to add more and more items into the system, including my retirement accounts, which consist of a variety of mutual funds. The program tracks my investment transactions and allows me to update my records with market prices, giving my retirement accounts a specific value.

This past weekend, I was back in my personal finance system entering check transactions, when it occurred to me that while I had the system open and the business section of the Saturday newspaper beside me, I ought to do some updating. I usually do this every two weeks, but for some reason, I hadn't updated my files in many weeks. I turned to the mutual fund section of the paper and began to locate my securities.

When I found the closing prices from the previous Friday, my lack of updated information began to make sense. During the month before, worldwide markets had been volatile, with Wall Street down roughly 20 percent from where it had been the month before. In fact, the market value of a number of my retirement accounts had drastically decreased. Hating to mentally accept the downturn in the market, I had employed a simple tactic— cling to yesterday's prices and leave the bad news alone. Pretend the market is still at its peak, and hope like crazy that sometime in the near future it will climb back to where it was.

While my action had not been deliberate, it illustrated to me how easy it is to gravitate to good news, markets that are up, and answers that are *yes*. And yet, it is often the downturns that make for great deals. When others sell and run, sales abound and opportunity knocks as never before.

By remaining stuck in July's news, albeit good news, I was missing the deals on the downside. Avoiding the bad news had caused me to miss good opportunities. Every disappointment, every downturn comes packed with lessons to learn. Clinging to yesterday always limits my investment in tomorrow. Don't avoid the bad times; build on them, learn from them, even go so far as to invest in them.

Have a great week.

A New Hammer

Greetings to you
this Monday morning.

For some time we have planned to finish off a portion of our basement to provide additional living space. This year, my New Year resolutions reflected this goal. Having spent the past few weeks with my tool belt in place, I now believe it might appear on next year's list as well. Nonetheless, I have enjoyed each small step forward.

This past weekend my father-in-law was in town and was curious to see what I was doing. After spending a few hours watching me swing my trusty old hammer, he disappeared to run some errands. Early in the afternoon, he appeared at the base of the stairs with his arm tucked behind his back. Proudly he presented me with a new yellow-handled hammer. "You need a heavier hammer to do the job you're working on," he explained. As I grasped the new tool, it was clear that the shiny head at the end of the yellow handle had significantly more substance than my old tool. I thanked him and went back to work.

For the balance of the weekend, I used my new hammer and noticed the following: the new tool was much more effective. Fewer strokes were needed to produce the same results. However, I hit my finger much more often with the new hammer than I did with my trusty old friend. There was pain associated with this newfound efficiency.

As with many things in life, swinging a new hammer can be a blend of pain and efficiency. The old way of doing things is familiar and comfortable. But as the task gets bigger and the nails get longer, a new hammer may be needed. Thumbs that always seemed to stay just outside of harm's way, suddenly find themselves in jeopardy. But through the pain we reach a new level of efficiency. We're better than we used to be.

Personally, I'm thankful that my father-in-law caused me a little pain over the weekend. I have hundreds of nails to drive in the next few months, and his advice will save me literally thousands of swings.

Don't be afraid to pick up a new tool. What you swing apprehensively today, you'll swing with confidence tomorrow. Whether it's a basement project or a relationship, we must be willing to endure the pain of today for the sake of tomorrow. It will be worth it.

Have a great week.

Hugs

F ew sports personalities have garnered more accolades and experienced more popularity that Michael Jordan of the Chicago Bulls™. And one evening not so long ago, as we watched, Michael once again showed why he is considered by many to be the best basketball player of all time.

MJ had just finished leading his team to their sixth NBA championship. He had once again taken the weight of the outcome on his own shoulders and delivered a victory in the manner to which we had become accustomed. At the sound of the last buzzer, the court flooded with members of the press, team personnel, and fans. Cameramen searched for just the right shot to capture the moment.

It didn't take long for them to find who they were looking for. They caught number 23 engaged in a congratulatory hug, his huge frame completely obscuring the image of the person he was hugging. Michael, oblivious to the attention, continued for an unusually long time. Finally, he stepped back and everyone realized that MJ was hugging his mother. This athletic icon, this man's man, this fierce competitor was basking in the tenderness and safety of a mother's hug.

This touching moment reminded me of another. Mary and I had joined with several others for a farewell sendoff. A friend of ours was leaving Kansas City for a year of military duty in Korea. During this time Kevin will be separated from his wife and three small children. As the evening came to a close, Kevin pulled me and two other dads aside and made one simple request. "I'd really appreciate it if you would hug Sam for me over the next year." Sam is Kevin's ten-year-old son. Kevin's love for Sam could extend over the thousands of miles between them but his arms could not. He was asking us to provide the arms. Kevin knew what a hug was worth.

You never outgrow a hug. You're never too old for one, never too small for one, and quite obviously, you're never too successful for one. When it's all said and done, sometimes a hug is more valuable than a championship ring.

"Yes Kevin, we'll be happy to see that Sam gets all the hugs he needs this next year."

Have a great week.

Clueless Keys

Greetings to you
this Monday morning.

Beside my sink in the bathroom of my home is a wooden contraption intended to hold loose change, a wallet, business cards, and other odds and ends that I take out of my pockets at the end of each day. The inventory of personal items seems to grow at a predictable rate, until I get to a place where I can either no longer stand to look at it, or items begin to spill out onto the vanity. Then I sort out the useless from the useful and begin again.

Over the weekend, as I was surveying the status of my collection contraption, I noticed a key that had been resting there for some time. It was a key without a ring, but it looked familiar. On closer inspection, I recognized it as the key to my 1985 Toyota™, which, of course, is no longer of any value to me because I no longer own the vehicle. Years before I had used the value of my Toyota™ to trade myself into something newer. As a result, I was left with a key and no car. This realization prompted me to look in our official key basket that sits by the back door in our kitchen. I wanted to see if we had any other useless keys. I was amazed to see that over time, we had collected a number of keys, many of which I could not even identify. No doubt somewhere there is a lock waiting to be opened, but the clueless key holder can't seem to match the problem with the answer.

What made this experience so poignant for me was that only hours before I had been in a conversation with one of my children about a certain problem he was encountering at school. I'm afraid that my initial reaction was to offer a solution, well before I'd understood the full extent of the present problem. My solution had served me well years before, but that didn't necessarily mean it would fit into the lock I was hearing about. In reality, it proved to be as useless as an old key. My key looked and sounded good, but unfortunately it didn't match the issue. I hadn't listened, and as such I missed a perfect opportunity to trade in what had worked for me yesterday for what could work for someone else today.

Have a great week.

Share the Soil

A couple of years ago I planted two ash trees in my backyard. The trees were roughly thirty feet apart and virtually the same height. I was pleased to see that both of the trees took root and grew in their first year. At the start of the second year, we built a flowerbed in the backyard that extended broadly enough to enclose one of the two ash trees. Because our backyard slopes away from the house, it was necessary to bring in rocks to edge the bed, along with a substantial amount of black dirt to fill in this area. From there we planted a variety of perennials and annuals.

As is often the case in Kansas City, we were forced to water this new area significantly during some of the hot, dry days of July and August. In the year that has followed, both our ash trees have stayed impeccably healthy, but the one in the newly formed flowerbed has grown roughly three feet more than its counterpart.

The attention and effort we directed toward the new plantings, combined with the extra soil we had hauled in, created a growing environment that far exceeded what we had offered our solo hardwood. Total autonomy had been replaced by companionship and an added depth that promoted growth at an accelerated rate.

The entire realization drew me to reconsider the value of something I've just begun doing with my children on a weekly basis. Each week I take one of them out for either breakfast or lunch. During that time we get updated on things that are going on in our lives. Included in the conversation that surrounds this meal is a time to ask some tough questions—the kind of questions that highlight the fact that my kids and I aren't alone. Questions that emphasize that the soil in which we grow, we also share.

There are times when growing alone and being fully autonomous sounds appealing. Independence can be elevated to a lofty level. However, the reality is that when we are planted next to others, we feed on each other, and accelerated growth results. So haul in some black dirt, buy some perennials, and stop trying to go it alone. July and August can be terribly hot and dry.

Have a great week.

Winding the Waterbury

Greetings to you
this Monday morning.

Last week, while entertaining at our home, one of the
guests looked at me and announced, "It's always 2:45
when we come to visit you." I gave him a questioning look.
Without a word he pointed to an antique wall clock that
hangs above our fireplace. A clock with a motionless
pendulum, a little hand pointing perpetually toward *two,*
and a big hand holding a silent vigil near the number
nine. "I've never seen it move," elaborated our visitor.

This is no ordinary clock. It had been purchased nearly
eighty years earlier by my grandfather as a gift to his local
country church. Several years ago, when a new church
building was built, the clock was given to me. It didn't
function properly at first, but I was able to find a clock-
master who was willing to work on it. So now, this stately
oak Waterbury wall clock hangs in poised position, ready
to serve the purpose for which it was created. And yet, it
continues to point at the *two* and the *nine,* forever

announcing that it is 2:45, waiting for me to take the time to do one important thing—wind it!

That's right. This finely tuned masterpiece won't function until I carefully open the glass front, insert the key, wind to the proper tension, and then prime the pendulum with the first swing. That would take only a few moments of my time and attention. But instead, it sits motionless, poised patiently, waiting for me to firmly and gently propel it back into action.

Like the Waterbury clock, there are people in my life who look to me for a little encouragement and attention. Their lives hold so much potential, so many finely tuned and precisely engineered skills and talents. Yet, I so easily walk past them day after day without noticing that they are frozen in place, unable to move on.

Are there people in your life who would be transformed into wonderful, contributing masterpieces if only you would take the time to nurture and encourage them? Don't allow them to continue to stand idle; do what you can to get them moving again, helping them fulfill the purpose for which they were created.

What time is it in your living room? Thankfully it's not 2:45 in mine anymore.

Have a great week.

Puddles

Greetings to you
this Monday morning.

I settled into my aisle seat for the ninety-minute trip to Minneapolis, only to find that I was sharing the row with two young boys and their overwhelmed mother. Two-year-old Tommy was the proud occupant of the window seat. His mother belted him in and he behaved like a perfect little gentleman for most of the flight. One-year-old Ryan, a reluctant resident of his mother's lap, was not quite as compliant.

As we began our descent, roughly twenty minutes before landing, Tommy started getting restless. Soon his quiet composure was gone and he burst into tears. Most likely, the descent had created a discomfort in his ears. For about five minutes, Tommy cried. The kind of cry that brings real tears. Tears that roll down cheeks with urgency. Then, as quickly as he started, Tommy stopped crying and slid back into his seat, belt in place, for the duration of the trip.

Several times I looked up from the book I was reading to see how he was doing. By this time he was well into the things that occupy the attention of a two-year-old boy. I couldn't help noticing, however, that situated right on top of his chubby two-year-old cheeks were two puddles—puddles filled with the tears he had only moments before cried. My first impulse was to reach over with my handkerchief and wipe them away, but for some reason, I hesitated. Tommy and his mom exchanged glances, but she didn't wipe away the puddles either. Instead they remained between blue eyes and rounded cheeks. A moment later, a broad smile burst across Tommy's face, but the puddles remained intact.

At that moment, I realized that my overriding tendency is to wipe the reminders of the past away and get on with today, especially when yesterday's memories are somehow associated with pain. Sunday I learned that sometimes it's okay to leave your handkerchief in your pocket. Sometimes it's good to leave the puddles, even to celebrate them. Puddles that make the smiles sweeter. Puddles that remind us that sadness doesn't last forever.

Don't be so quick to wipe away the puddles.

Have a great week.

The Catcher's Mitt

For Christmas one year, Mary and I bought our son Erik an expensive catcher's mitt. It was a beautiful tan leather, with the appropriate padding, pocket, and stitching.

Erik used the mitt for friendly games of backyard ball, but despite its quality, the mitt had one frustrating characteristic—its rigid form made it hard to squeeze. More often than not, the ball would hit the center of the mitt and pop back out. Erik never really complained, he just used our gift less and less.

When spring swung around, Erik signed up for Little League baseball. When asked what position he preferred, catcher was at the top of his list. With sincere delight, his coach, Bob Jones, informed him that he too had played catcher, most recently in the minor leagues with the Chicago White Sox™.

A short time later, Bob complimented me on the mitt we had chosen for Erik, but then sheepishly asked if he could borrow it for the weekend. "It needs a proper "break-in treatment," he explained.

A few days later, he pulled the mitt from his duffel bag and handed it to Erik. It was folded in half, still tied tightly with strings. He carefully cut the strings that held it shut, exposing a wrapped baseball that had been held inside. Once the ball was removed, we could see that the center of the mitt was now darkened and oily, but Erik didn't seem to mind. He quickly slid his twelve-year-old hand inside the glove and began to open and close the mitt. No words were necessary; his eyes said it all, and in that instant, Bob knew he had done his job. In one weekend, the process had converted a picture-perfect mitt into a user-friendly mitt, a rigid form into a pliable tool.

Simply stated, resist the urge to maintain an image that's attractive, untouched, rigid and useless. Opt instead to let life's experiences soften you into a pliable, useful, and seasoned individual. One looks good on the shelf; the other works good in the game.

Life will throw you curve balls in the dirt. A soft, well-oiled, broken-in individual can scoop it up and go on. That's called character, and that's what separates the guys on the bench from the guys in the game.

Have a great week.

Life Is a Classroom

Greetings to you
this Monday morning.

Last week I made my lunch-hour trek back to the Community Blood Center for my regular donation. By this point I have the routine down—which forms must be read, which questions must be answered, which finger they will stick, and most importantly, which cookies taste the best.

After the preliminaries were complete, I made my way to the reclining chair/bed where the pint of blood is drawn. I stood beside the brown vinyl recliner while the nurse inspected my arms and informed me that she would like to use my left arm. Then she asked me a question that made me shudder. "Would you mind being my first patient?" *First patient?* This was her first day on duty, and as a result, she had an experienced nurse at her side throughout the procedure. Politeness overwhelmed honesty, and I agreed to let her train on my left arm.

For the next half-hour, this nurse-trainee moved exceptionally slow and tentatively. She scrubbed nearly all of my left arm, covered me with paper aprons, "just in case," and constantly poked at the vein. Then she dutifully and somewhat apologetically informed me that there would be a "little stick," and there was. At that point, her teacher moved to the forefront to inspect the work and make a few alterations that immediately improved blood flow and comfort level. In detail, her teacher explained the changes she would make, and told her how she could improve her technique with the next donor. In that moment, I had become a training exhibit, a practice patient, a textbook with real veins.

Perhaps someday, that young nurse will train others from the confident expertise she learned while reluctantly experimenting on my left arm. Perhaps someday she might even save a life with the skill that I helped her develop.

Each day we are given new opportunities to help others learn. Your willingness to endure the discomfort, tolerate the delays, and smile through the pokes, serves as a gift to someone who is trying to master a skill.

Life is a classroom. Sometimes you're the student, sometimes you're the teacher, and sometimes you're the assignment. I'm glad that through the years, people have given me their left arms to practice on. Last week it was my turn.

Have a great week.

"You're the One"

Christmas Eve at King's College in Cambridge, England, is a special and eagerly anticipated time, for on that night each year the King's youth choir performs its famous Christmas concert.

All the choir members are gifted vocalists, but a significant part of the Christmas concert is the performance of a young soloist. This lad, whoever he is, must perform in front of a huge audience packing the cathedral and the hundreds of thousands in the remote worldwide television audience beyond the stone walls. This would be a daunting task for even the most experienced performer, let alone a child. However, the directors at King's College have devised a tried-and-true strategy for producing a successful concert.

Quite simply, it boils down to this. All the boys in the choir learn the solo passages; all are equally prepared. Then, thirty seconds before the concert begins, moments before the cameras go live, the conductor taps one boy on the shoulder and announces, "You're the one."

When I visited Cambridge, a guide explained the rationale behind this selection process. "The young performer is spared from the worry that often accompanies a prospect of such significance, and he is kept from getting a big head," he told us. It's easy enough to see how this strategy would preserve the key elements that continue to make the concert an annual event not to be missed.

Perhaps the folks at King's College have discovered something that would work in other areas of life. Various sections of your local bookstore contain volumes promising the keys to success. But the real key may be the attitude of the heart. Time management, strategic planning, and decision-making all have their places. Yet when preparation and humility meet opportunity, everyone benefits—no matter who gets the recognition.

The directors at King's College Choir have uncovered a method that annually leads to success. We must each find our own strategy for keeping our attitudes straight and performances honest and pure. It should be something that is decided on long before the performance begins, something that gives us a little tap on the shoulder and reminds us to say "no" to pride and "yes" to well-practiced opportunity.

Have a great week.

Vacation

Greetings to you
this Monday morning.

Mountains of sand and miles of beach at the Michigan Dunes. A shared back seat with my twin sister, Debbie, constantly crossing that imaginary line into "my space." Endless games of "Authors," invoking such memorable lines as, "Do you have Louisa May Alcott's, *Little Women?*"

Back then, vacation was something I did. Now, as a husband and father, vacations are something I create, adding my own special images and perspective. These days, it's my responsibility to orchestrate the customs and activities that will plant precious memories in my children's minds.

Days of maneuvering around strategically placed staging areas, in anticipation of loading and departure: sleeping bags over there, water toys and swimming suits over here, snacks there, cassette tapes here. Neighbors to contact, a dog to board, a map to ponder, and don't forget to stop the newspaper. A last-minute trip to fill the gas tank and pick up cash at the ATM. Then the big moment arrives.

The 4:00 A.M. alarm sounds, the van and its white bubble carrier top are loaded, and we are soon on our way to McDonald's™ for the annual celebration breakfast, marking the official launching of a new vacation. There is nothing quite as sweet as the feeling I get as I pull out of the driveway while the rest of the neighborhood is fast asleep, knowing that for the next two weeks, I can devote myself to rest, relaxation, and renewal. The phone won't ring and the system won't crash. Routine and pressure can be set aside for family and fun.

The *American Heritage Dictionary* defines *vacation* as "A period of time devoted to pleasure, rest, or relaxation, especially one with pay granted to an employee." A period of time that's often hard to squeeze in. A period of time that takes resources that could easily be used for other things. A period of time I need.

I want my kids to know me in shorts as well as a suit. I want time with them when my biggest decision is whether to "leave the Queen of Diamonds or pick up the top card." I want to pose for corny pictures, eat cookies for breakfast, and walk barefoot until noon. I want to laugh with my kids and go to bed before they do.

My alarm is set for 4:00 A.M.

Have a great week.

Growth Rings

Greetings to you
this Monday morning.

Several years ago I removed a number of damaged, unhealthy trees from our backyard. After I had completed the cutting and clearing, I went back and took a closer look at the stumps and made a fascinating discovery.

The growth rings of the trees were so clearly visible that I could count them. I could also read the story they told. Each ring was distinctly separate yet linked to the core of the previous years. Each ring had a different width, depending on whether the growing season had been good or bad. And with each passing year, the rings became larger and stronger.

This past weekend as we celebrated my parents' sixtieth wedding anniversary, I was reminded of the trees and their distinctive rings. I couldn't help thinking that our family tree has many things in common with the trees from my backyard. From those first two, my father and mother, our family has grown to forty-four. Yet my parents, both over eighty, remain the core strength, the inspiration, around which each subsequent ring has grown. All of us are indelibly marked by yesterday, even though we require nourishment from today.

There have been good years and bad years, dry times and abundant times. Only yesterday my kids were the outside ring. Now, another generation encircles them. The children of yesterday have become the parents of today, and the parents of yesterday are the grandparents of today. And each generation is indebted to and linked to the solid core provided by my parents.

Strong trees survive. They bask in the sunshine, drink in the rain, and stand firm and sure in stormy weather. Strong trees thrive, each new ring supported by the strength of the past.

Strong families survive and thrive as well, supported by the core of the older generations. The young rings of today are forever linked with the aging rings of yesterday. And before you know it, you're closer to the core than to the outside edge.

Count the rings in your life. Take your place seriously. Grow a family tree.

Have a great week.

An Extra Squeeze

Whenever I drink grapefruit juice for breakfast, I am transported back to my childhood. As soon as that tart citrus bursts against my tongue, I remember the grapefruit halves my mother used to serve me with my eggs or my cereal.

With the narrow, serrated spoon she placed beside my plate, I would do my best to extract each pale yellow segment. Then, with the scooping work done, I would squeeze the remaining juice from the empty peel. Squeeze. Fill the little spoon. Drink that wonderful fresh liquid. Squeeze again.

When I was finished, my mother would always ask, "Have you squeezed all the juice out of your grapefruit?" And I always answered confidently that I had. But she wasn't about to take my word for it. Not when she knew it was still loaded with "good stuff." I would watch with amazement as she picked up the smashed yellow carcass I had left and squeeze out spoonful after spoonful!

Last week, this memory from my childhood flashed across my mind as I stood beside my wife's hospital bed, waiting for the nurses to wheel her into surgery. Tears welled up in both our eyes as we silently contemplated the agonizing uncertainty of that moment. I suddenly thought about all the juice I'd failed to squeeze out of the opportunities life had afforded us. In slow motion, my thoughts panned across the words I'd left unsaid, the things I'd left undone, the time I'd wasted. I knew that somehow I had failed to squeeze every last drop of joy out of the life we'd been given, and now I so badly wanted the opportunity to try again.

Life, like the grapefruit, is filled with nourishment, flavor, and richness. More often than not, however, it takes an extra squeeze or two to extract every drop of its delicious juice. That is often an extra squeeze of commitment, determination, and priority. A squeeze that shows you're willing to work harder and spend more time capturing every drop.

Are you getting all that life has to offer you? Take an extra squeeze.

Have a great week.

Letting Go

Last week, I was once again in my basement, this time constructing a shower. As part of this process, I pieced together rigid material that made up the wall unit. Unlike much of the work I have done before, this material had to be secured to the surface behind it with a very strong adhesive. The challenge of the adhesive is that it takes some time to fully set, and as a result, I had to find a way to hold it in place while it hardened.

For small pieces I used masking tape. For larger pieces, I used blocks of wood leveraged against the wall on the other side. In all instances, I did my best to make certain the location was correct and the leveling was optimal before putting the supports in place. Twenty-four hours later, as I removed the supports, everything remained securely in place.

While I was busy installing the shower, my two boys were working on the ceiling insulation. I couldn't help but notice how self-sufficient, independent, and confident they had become. What a contrast to the years when nearly every chore was accompanied by a string of questions.

As I worked, I began to realize that the process I was going through installing the shower is similar to the process I am going through with my children. As a parent, I have been working hard to see that the components and pieces of their lives are properly set in place. While the adhesive is still very soft, much of my time is taken up with supporting these elements—checking to make certain things are level here and snug there. All of this time and effort built upon the hope that when the tape and braces are one day removed, my children will stand firm in the values they have been taught and remain balanced in their approach to life.

I've learned that removing the supports too early can have serious consequences. I've also learned that waiting too long can sometimes create a dependence on the tape and braces that can make it difficult to ever remove them.

I'm thankful for the people in my life who held me firmly to the principles that today have become my own. I'm also thankful that at some point they let go.

Have a great week.

No Shortcuts for Champions

L ast weekend I watched a baseball game on television while I worked on a couple of projects in my basement. As the game moved along, I began to notice one particular commercial that aired every few innings.

The commercial, marketing a breakfast cereal, was offering a sleeve of golf balls for three box tops. What I found so strange about the commercial was that it made a phenomenal claim. If I would include this cereal as a regular part of my diet and use the brand of golf balls specified, I could be just like the famous young golfer Tiger Woods. *Imagine!*

That promise rolled over in my mind for the rest of the afternoon. No doubt certain aspects of the commercial were true. I don't doubt that Tiger Woods eats the high-powered flakes for breakfast on occasion or that he tees up with that particular brand of golf balls, but even if I do the same, how could that make me *just like* Tiger?

Not that it wouldn't be great. Three-hundred-yard drives, pinpoint-accurate fairway irons, and a steady putting hand, all the result of an early morning menu change and the purchase of top quality golf balls. *How absurd!* Tiger Woods hasn't risen to the top in the game of golf by using a particular brand of golf ball or eating a certain type of breakfast food. It has taken talent, determination, and years of dedicated practice.

This oversimplification made me think about the people in my life that I respect and admire. People I'd love to be more like. I often find myself captivated by their success, their prominence, their skills, and their reputations. But I know there are no shortcuts to being like them. No diets to change, no golf balls to buy. Instead, it will take practice, commitment, heart, sacrifice, and humility.

Who do you want to be like? What champion do you want to emulate? Figure out what makes that person work on the inside before you worry about the externals. There are no shortcuts for champions.

Have a great week.

"Fog"

After a full day of activity in London, I headed for my lodgings. The traffic on the M25 was moderate, and my exit to the M20 was just twenty miles ahead. Things were looking good when suddenly I hit a wave of fog that lasted only a few seconds. Shortly after that I hit another wave, and soon the intermittent waves had become a consistent shroud that forced me to slow my pace considerably. The further I drove, the tighter the fog gripped the unfamiliar roadway.

The tighter the fog gripped the road, the tighter I gripped the steering wheel and peered intently into the pea soup. The density of the fog made the road signs indecipherable until I was almost on top of them. Finally, with shoulder muscles tense and aching, my senses almost dull from focusing so hard, I spotted four sets of blinking yellow lights in the distance. I slowed down even more, uncertain of what they meant, but hoping they would provide direction.

As I drew closer, I could see that the lights were road signs that pulsated in unison, shining forth with one word of warning to highway travelers: "FOG." I groaned in disappointment at this useless statement of the obvious. There were no flashing lights offering direction. No promises of assistance. Just "FOG." Nothing but pointless signs announcing what everyone on the road already knew. An unmistakable exclamation point behind the problem, but no help for the present or hope for the future.

Stating the obvious is easy. It's also useless. It's energy wasted, energy that should be spent illuminating the road ahead. Many along life's pathway are willing to tell us the obvious about the past or the present. The helpful ones are those who will illuminate and expose, those who will risk and accompany, those who will dream and develop. The first are critics; the second are friends.

A true friend does more than tell us we're lost. A true friend helps us find our way home.

Have a great week.

Something to Grip

Never before had I witnessed a varsity high school basketball game that was terminated before the final buzzer. A week ago at a school just south of Kansas City, I was present for just such an occasion.

The teams came ready to play, and all indications were that they would do just that. But as the game moved along, we noticed that the floor of the gymnasium was glistening and unusually slick. Because our pre-game drive had been accompanied by snowfall, we assumed that moisture had been tracked in on the shoes of fans. Several times during the contest, the lead referee stopped play and asked for a towel to wipe up a particularly slippery area. But as the game progressed, conditions worsened.

By the start of the fourth quarter, many of the players had literally slipped and fallen at least once. With five minutes to go, the referee had seen enough. He motioned to the scorer's table and ended the game.

As we made our way out of the facility, an embarrassed school administrator apologetically explained the situation. Earlier in the day, in anticipation of the pending contest, the school had commissioned the floor to be waxed. Because a step in the process had been skipped, the floor was beautiful, but unusable. Young men who typically moved with power and confidence were forced to play with less intensity and consequently, less skill. The dynamics of the game were completely changed.

The situation made me think of times when I've described a relationship as having lost some of its luster— times when I've felt as though my shine had worn off a little with my wife, my kids, my friends, or my work colleagues. Generally I consider such a condition to be negative, yet as I think about it, that may not be the case. The worn places are not as slick as a newly waxed floor would be, allowing for a better grip. As I reveal more of who I really am, the shine may be diminished, but the traction is greatly improved.

Often the things that seem to shine the brightest provide little to hang on to. Better to have a low-luster finish and a firm grip. It gives those around you the opportunity to play at their best. Be real. Set the wax aside.

Have a great week.

"This End Up"

Several recent purchases have focused my attention on a particular external label found on many boxes. Frequently there is a message in bold and unmistakable letters on the exterior of the box, accompanied by a simple graphic design. The notification to which I'm referring is "This end up." More often than not, an arrow points in the appropriate direction to fully illustrate the proper placement of the contents and the position for opening.

At times the rationale for this directive isn't clear until the box is opened. But disregarding it always leads to chaos. I have on occasion opened the wrong end only to find loose parts and breakable components spilling out in a confused mess. That can make the task of assembly far more difficult.

The impact of my "this end up" experience hit me as I was sitting in a Kansas City high school gymnasium for the fourth time in a week. I watched with interest and enthusiasm as my sons played in two basketball games. This activity had been a far cry from the demands and dictates of an over-full work week. I had been stretched in more ways than I cared to recount. The pages of my planner were full of action items and follow-up assignments. The moments away from the job were saturated with thoughts of pending promises and overdue commitments.

In the middle of all of the pulls and tugs, I found myself captivated by the joy of watching my boys, ages fifteen and seventeen, running full speed up and down a hardwood floor. *This is the part of my life that belongs on the top,* I thought. This was the end I wanted up. These were the loose and fragile pieces that are too easily lost or broken if they're allowed to fall under the load of other pressures.

I quickly resolved that from that day on, I would stop and read the box first, always noting the living reminders of which way the arrow is pointing.

"This end up!" It's the only way to preserve the precious and often fragile parts of your life.

Have a great week.

Eye-to-Eye

Recently I made my way to a local bookstore to get caught up on some Christmas shopping. As I entered the store, I noticed that one of my shoelaces was untied. I bent down, tied my shoe, and looked up directly into the eyes of an eighteen-month-old boy. I was startled; he was delighted. Another set of eyes at his level was cause for celebration, and his face demonstrated his excitement.

I was so taken back that I stood to my feet and began to walk away, until my heart compelled me to do otherwise. I crouched down once again, and this time I spoke a greeting to the little stranger. Once again, he smiled with delight at the unexpected eye contact and my friendly words.

In the crowd, this young lad's view had primarily been kneecaps and coattails. He was virtually invisible among the shopping throng, except for the top of his little head and the flash of his yellow snowsuit. Yet, in one unexpected instant, he had someone to connect with—someone to look at eye-to-eye.

Later, as I thought about the encounter, I began to realize something about myself. I thought about how easy it is for me to miss many of the searching eyes that cross my path, perhaps some in my own family. I'm too busy to stop, let alone bend over and make eye contact. Consequently I miss those impromptu opportunities that life affords. Instead I'm content to look at the tops of heads and the blur of yellow as life races by.

I doubt I will ever see that young boy again. However, the reminder he left me will last a long time. I don't want people to simply recognize my kneecaps and coattails. I want them to see my eyes because that's the only way for our hearts to touch.

The next time your view changes, enjoy it. Take time to see what the world looks like from that perspective. You might just catch a pair of eyes that you've been overlooking, a pair of eyes that need a heart to connect with.

Have a great week.

Push, Don't Pamper

Greetings to you
this Monday morning.

While a senior at Taylor University, I was part of an outstanding wrestling team. Our success was due in large part to a teammate named Glenn Guerin, who as a junior, had become Taylor's first national champion.

Glenn wrestled in the 126-pound weight class. Because I had passed that weight class long before, I was never matched up against Glenn in drills or live action. That is until one day when many of my teammates were out of town for the holidays. With few options, my coach was forced to pair me off with Glenn. I remember the fear and caution that dominated each of my moves. I wasn't afraid for my own health and safety but rather that I might do the unthinkable—hurt our champion.

I could picture myself going down in Taylor annuls as the blundering practice partner who wrestled the national champ and fell on his hand, twisted his knee, or injured him in some critical way that cost Glenn his senior year.

As a result, I turned in a very cautious and uninspired performance.

After about ten minutes of this lackluster action, the silence was broken by a sharp and unmistakable sound—coach Jarman's whistle. Without hesitation, he pointed at me and hollered, "You're afraid you're going to hurt him, aren't you?" I was shocked at his perception. Had it been that obvious? Before I could answer, he continued, "You'll hurt him for sure if you don't push him enough to make him a better wrestler. If you protect him and refuse to go all out, you'll kill his chance to repeat!"

It hadn't occurred to me that if I performed at my best, I could contribute to the making of a champion. By risking, challenging, and pushing my teammate, I could help him reach his fullest potential.

Challenge those you care about to improve and grow. Do it carefully, thoughtfully, and honestly. Conversely, take the constructive criticism of others as an opportunity to learn and refine your own skills. Don't pamper each other into mediocrity.

By the way, Glenn did repeat as national champion. He did it by pushing himself. He did it because his teammates pushed him as well. Including me.

Have a great week.

Making a Break for It

On a typical Saturday at our house, I go in and out of the garage for a variety of reasons. Each time I exit, I hit the garage door opener button located by our back door. The noise inevitably inspires our ten-year-old dog, Mackie, to bolt through the back door and race at breakneck speed for the slowly elevating door. Sometimes she actually outruns the pace at which the door is being lifted and is forced to squeeze through the narrow space. This is not a new practice for Mackie. Ever since she arrived at our house, she has made a habit of dashing when the garage door opens.

Each time she immerges on the other side of the garage door, she prances around in anticipation. She looks side to side fully expecting a surprise or challenge to be waiting for her. From time to time, she is rewarded with a squirrel to chase, a rabbit to race, or a visitor to greet. But most often, Mackie is confronted with the same slab of concrete, the same shrubs, and the same view as the time before. Yet, with unwavering enthusiasm when the garage door goes up, she goes out, ears up, tail wagging, feet flying, as happy as a pup.

I don't know much about a dog's psyche. This behavior could easily be written off to a very short memory or limited intelligence. But whatever the logical explanation, the practical lesson has become obvious to me. What if every experience in my life evoked this degree of enthusiasm? What if every time the door was raised on a new day, a new project, a new experience, or even the same old ones, I raced at breakneck speed to greet the opportunity? What if I met tomorrow's familiar slab of concrete with a tail in full wag and feet that pranced?

What if there was a squirrel to chase or a rabbit to race, but I never made a break for it? The door on today has been open for only a few hours, and the promise of tomorrow is just around the corner. Sprint to it.

Have a great week.

Get the
Recipe

Several days ago, while Mary and I were attending a retreat, I had occasion to sample some homemade cookies that I found on a snack table. The fact that I found my way to the cookie area is no real surprise, but my particular fondness for the variety in question was. You see, I usually prefer chocolate and these were molasses cookies.

When Mary noticed how much I was enjoying these treats, she asked around until she found out who had brought them. A few minutes later she was conversing with the baker in question and discussing the fine points of her creation.

Although I enjoyed that little caloric indulgence, I've given little thought to it since. That is, until this past weekend when we received a gift from the baker of those treats. An electronic mail arrived, which contained the list of ingredients, the mixing order, and the baking instructions for those outstanding cookies.

While receiving a fresh batch of the cookies would have been of more immediate value, having the recipe now provides an opportunity that extends well beyond the immediate. Now the access to this treat is within my grasp. The recipe is ours.

Throughout my life I have had opportunity to be impacted in dramatic ways by a wide variety of people. In the process, I have been impressed, challenged, and at times, entertained. In most cases, as time has moved me further from the event or the individual, the significance of the experience has faded. Seldom have I had the insight, wisdom, or courage to ask for the recipe—an answer that might have extended the taste of the initial encounter for years and impacted me well beyond the experience itself.

From cookies to life, the parallel is clear. When you taste or experience something you enjoy and respect, get the recipe. Ask the question. Take the time. There is no greater compliment to the baker, the parent, the sibling, or the friend than to ask for the secret to their success.

Why just snack on a cookie or two when you can have the recipe? Before the memory fades, ask for it.

Have a great week.

Leaky Faucets

Nearly twenty years ago, as Mary and I were shopping for our first home, I remember the realtor showing us a property that she termed "charming." That, as I later learned, means old and requiring lots of time and money. Over the next seven years, we poured plenty of both into this house.

One of the first problems we faced was poor water pressure. When the house was constructed, lead and galvanized steel pipes were used throughout. Over the years, the flow of water was slowed by growing corrosion. That, along with the health implications, prompted corrective action.

On the day the new pipes were being installed, we turned off the water to the house until the work was done. Once the water was flowing again, I noticed that faucets were leaking. This surprised me because they had been working fine before we turned the water off. The fixtures that previously had only been required to restrain a marginal flow of water were now straining to accommodate the added water pressure. The successful correction of one problem had created another problem down the line.

Over time I've discovered this same principal at work in my everyday life. A determination to improve in one area brings increased enthusiasm, commitment, and drive. This shifts the focus of the pressure more squarely onto other aspects of life.

Did those leaky faucets mean that replacing the pipes wasn't worthwhile? Not at all. In fact, it meant that I was one step closer to solving the entire problem. In clear terms, I was reminded that newly discovered drips shouldn't always be interpreted as a failure. In reality it was one of the clearest indications that I had solved the problem I set out to fix.

When you determine to fix something, don't expect a single effort to solve the whole problem. It may just serve to move the spotlight to the next problem along the line. With my new pipes in, it was time to learn how to replace worn and tired washers—a skill I would never have learned if I had been satisfied with mediocre performance.

Don't be afraid to spring a few leaks. Instead celebrate the milestone it represents.

Have a great week.

A Stiff Southerly Breeze

Greetings to you this Monday morning.

One evening last week as I exited the front door of our offices, I was greeted by a strong, steady, southerly wind. I made my way to our family van and began my eight-mile journey home. For the first part of my commute, I was headed directly into the wind. I could literally feel the resistance to my van's forward motion. On the second half, the wind pounded against the left side of the van, making it more difficult to guide my vehicle along in a straight line. As I drove through rush-hour traffic, I was amazed by this constant and powerful force.

Not too far from my home, I drove by a local business that was proudly displaying an American flag on a pole in front of the main entrance. What was noteworthy about this sight was the way the flag stood out perfectly straight. The same wind that made my driving difficult, provided a picture-perfect display of our nation's true colors. It was that unfurled flag that drove home a point that evening.

I prefer light, gentle breezes or no resistance at all as I move through life and the experiences that each new day brings. I want the pushback to be held to a minimum. My tendency is to find the path of least resistance and go. Yet the same wind that at times makes forward progress more difficult, also has as a byproduct—the ability to force flags to unfurl and colors to show.

When the way is easy and the wind is calm, nearly every flag looks the same, but with increased velocity comes a fuller picture of individual character. Each stripe, each star, each pattern is fully revealed in the face of growing velocity.

When the wind blows strong, the journey gets tougher; but there is more opportunity than ever to show your true colors to the world around you. Don't begrudge the wind. Put it to work for you. Use it to prove your character and show the colors of your flag.

Have a great week.

They're Watching

This past weekend I transported a group of high school boys to a basketball game in which they were competing. Our destination was roughly a two-hour drive.

It was a fine day to travel—clear roads and bright skies. In fact, by the time I'd pulled our family van into the school parking lot, the bright midday skies were beckoning me to take a short sun induced nap. The boys quickly hopped out of the vehicle with gym bags in tow, but Alli, my eleven-year-old daughter, was not so anxious to make her way to the rigid, backless, and unforgiving wooden benches. She opted to pull out a book she was working through. I made my napping intentions known to her and checked my clock. I had just enough time for a nap before the start of the first game. I reclined the driver's seat and quickly drifted off.

I was sound asleep, basking in the warmth of the sun's rays, when suddenly I was jarred awake by a loud noise. I looked around, trying to identify the sound, but all I saw were the eyes of my eleven-year-old looking at me in absolute amazement. I situated myself again and had just dosed off when the noise woke me again. Just as before, I glanced back and saw my daughter's amused face. Slightly embarrassed but chuckling, I realized I had literally snored myself awake.

What stuck with me that day was the observant, amazed, entertained, and fully engaged eyes of my daughter. Alli was paying attention to me. She was watching, listening, and ingesting all that took place. In her own way, she was giving me notice that she pays attention. Saturday I entertained and humored her; sometimes I mentor and guide; other times I disappoint and discourage. In each case, she is paying attention.

Who watches you? Who pays attention when you snore? If you're like me, someone whom you care deeply about probably has his or her eyes focused in your direction. I won't soon forget those two beautiful eyes that gave me notice Saturday. I'm being watched.

Have a great week.

Building on the Ashes

With the onset of crisp fall mornings has come the urge to have a fire in the fireplace. However, before a log can be placed on the grate, the task of cleaning out last year's ashes has to be completed. With a paper grocery bag by my side and the little fireplace shovel in my hand, I begin the tedious task of scooping and dumping. With the fireplace now empty, I carefully remove the ash-filled bag and safely tuck it away in the garage.

With a clean fireplace, I am ready for action, or am I? Over the years I've learned something about clean fireplaces. While they may look nicer, they don't seem to function quite as well. With all the old ashes removed, the fresh hot coals fall from the grate to the concrete below, a full three to four inches below the wood that is waiting to be burned. The distance makes it more difficult to keep the fire burning strong.

After some ash has accumulated, the hot coals fall into the elevated bed, closer to the logs they are intended to consume. The result is a fire that is larger and easier to maintain. Ash, the residue of the past, now supports the coals of the present.

Over time, we all accumulate our share of ash. Some is the product of planning and pleasure, and some is produced by mistakes and pain. Some comes from laughter, and some comes from tears. Some is the result of one dynamic event, and some results from the rigors of daily life.

We often feel the need to shovel the past away, to start fresh and clean. From the best of intentions we scoop and fill and dispose of as much of what we don't want from the past as possible. The past, like ash, is impossible to ignite again. Yet, when properly considered, the past provides the bed upon which the coals of our present passions and dreams rest.

Resist the urge to pour the past into the landfill of regret and denial. Instead let the embers of today lay upon the ash of yesterday. The fire will be hotter, and the results will be more dramatic. Bask in the warmth of today's fire, fueled by the hopes and dreams of tomorrow, resting upon the results of yesterday.

Have a great week.

The Border

Greetings to you
this Monday morning.

Just over four months ago, anticipating an upcoming visit from Mary's parents, she and I decided to redo our laundry room. This is a small room with a high ceiling, tucked inconspicuously in a corner spot between our garage and kitchen. I chose the paint and Mary ordered a lovely wallpaper border to go around the top as a perfect accent.

I finished the painting on the final weekend before our visitors were to arrive. All that remained was to apply the twenty-eight-plus feet of wallpaper border. We were disappointed to learn, however, that the border would not arrive for another week. To make matters worse, I had left a three-inch unpainted stripe at the top of each wall in anticipation of the wallpaper I was expecting to hang.

Our guests came and went, and no one commented on the unfinished state of our laundry room. My personal belief is that not one of them even stepped foot inside the room during the visit. A week later, Mary picked up the delinquent order and placed the two small rolls in the laundry room, where they sat untouched for months.

Last weekend, I unwrapped the rolls of border, dragged a stepladder into the awkward space, and finished the job. Less than an hour later, I stood surveying the results and wondering why I had bothered. After all, no one had noticed when it was partially done, and no one would notice now. Just as I finished, Mary appeared in the doorway and scanned the room in quiet evaluation. The silence was broken with two simple observations. "Wow, this really looks good," she said in acknowledgment of the appropriate color selection and pattern. Then she followed with the payoff, "This will really make it nicer to do the laundry."

There it was. I'd avoided the task for four months, convinced that it wouldn't matter to anyone. Convinced that no one would notice. I was nearly right. But, that one exception was significant. That one exception was enough to make the effort worthwhile.

Sometimes the notice given for the tasks we complete is substantial. At other times, the only reason we do what we do is to make it nicer for the person who does the laundry. And that's most definitely reason enough.

Have a great week.

Stumbling
Into
Opportunity

I knew I had seen the book I wanted just a few days before. I checked my usual storage spots, but to no avail. So I employed the mental exercise that begins with the sentence, "Now, where did I see it last?" After a few minutes of pondering, I convinced myself that I had last seen my paperback on the floor of our family van.

With confidence, I pulled open the driver's-side door and quickly scanned the small carpeted area between the two front seats—nothing. Glove compartments—nothing. Then it occurred to me to check under the driver's seat. I wedged my left hand under the seat and began to blindly explore. My fingers moved side to side, groping for my lost treasure, until it struck something. I knew immediately that it was a book, but not my book. Hard cover versus paperback. Too big—considerably more than my 125-page novel I was trying to track down. I pulled the book out from under the seat and noted the plastic cover and familiar tag identifying it as a library book.

With the newly retrieved book in tow, I marched back into the house and encountered Alli, who commented with great enthusiasm, "Wow Dad, where did you find Erik's book? Mom's been looking all over the house for that!" Moments later I offered the book to Erik, who responded with no less amazement.

It seemed that while pursuing my own agenda, I'd stumbled directly into somebody else's. In an instant, I had become a local hero, simply because I'd been looking in the wrong place at the right time. Discovery often works that way. You start looking with a particular end in mind, and along the way you find what you hadn't even been smart enough to look for. Opportunity opens at times, even before you knock.

It's never bad to search for what you cannot find, but never overlook the opportunity that comes from discovering what you had no idea you were looking for. Sometimes stumbling into the profound is of far more value than locating the mundane.

Have a great week.

Making Stars of Spectators

Greetings to you
this Monday morning.

I 've made my share of visits to the lovely city of Munich. There are so many things that I have come to love and expect each time I visit. The wonderful Bavarian food, the orderly and carefully cared for environment, the punctual trains, trams and buses, the classic old as well as the new high-tech architecture all provide a much-appreciated experience.

In the heart of Munich is an area where I love to walk. It's known as the Marienplatz and contains both shops and tourist landmarks. Without exception, the area is full of people eating, shopping, snapping pictures, and some just observing. Over the years, I've seen a wide variety of local and international entertainers performing in the Marienplatz. Each is seeking a bit of pocket cash and applause.

Last week, as I was making my way back to my hotel, I came across the largest crowd I have ever seen watching such a performance. Observers had formed a large circle four and five deep. The entertainer was interacting with the crowd, randomly extracting observers to act out a script. In addition to those with acting parts, the performer had the vast audience providing sound effects, cheering, and laughter on his cue. Finally, when the volunteer actors had been properly prepared for their respective roles, the performer waved them into action and pretended to be the cameraman filming the production. There were great cheers, roars, and applause as the action came to a halt. All who observed had most definitely been entertained, myself included.

What struck me profoundly was the difference between this performance and any other I had observed in the Marienplatz. Rather than highlighting individual accomplishment, this performer had simply made stars out of the unassuming and untrained, and participants out of observers. His job was to make sure that we, the audience, entertained each other. He did it to perfection. So much so, that when the show was over, he simply took his hat off and stood quietly as people came forward to contribute their tangible appreciation for his efforts.

In this day when individual performance seems to be highly valued, don't underestimate the merit of coaching, serving, conducting, and directing others into greatness. The spotlight doesn't have to be on you for the experience to be rewarding. Make somebody a star.

Have a great week.

Complete But Hidden

Last night, as I was driving home from work, I saw an incredible sight. Perfectly framed in the darkening sky was a sliver of light. The moon. Although it was beautiful, I couldn't help remembering only days earlier when it had been bold and unmistakable—a full circle of light, impressive to all beholders. What I saw last night was humbler and less apparent, yet every bit as awesome.

Upon closer observation, I noticed that the entire moon was in fact still visible if I looked ever so carefully. The faint outline of the remainder of the vast object now lay in the shadows, but it could be seen. The impatient observer might have concluded that the moon itself had mysteriously changed shape over the course of a few days. In reality, the focus of the light had changed and the full image was now hidden. It was still there, waiting for its moment in the light once again. Complete but hidden, awesome but obscure.

I was left thinking about how closely this parallels life. There are days when we have our moment in the light. There are other days when only those who look closely can see the entire scope of our beauty. On the hidden days, we are completely present as always, just less visible, more easily overlooked. No matter how full we appear to others, we should go about our lives with the confident assurance of our fullness. For as certainly as more of the moon will be exposed in the nights to come, so too, we will have intervals of more intense illumination. Our moments in the shadows keep us humble and pressing on, while our moments in the light serve to give us purpose and confidence. Both serve us well in the cycles of our lives.

Regardless of where you currently find yourself, remember that both the shadow and the light have their purpose. Learn to value both. Be content to wait patiently for your day in the light and rest securely as you encounter the shadows. You will be better for it.

Have a great week.

Another Stage

Greetings to you
this Monday morning.

I 'd just finished one last glimpse at the famous Tower of London and now headed into the London Underground to purchase my ticket to Marble Arch, a landmark close to my hotel. With ticket firmly in hand, I made my way toward the enormous escalator that leads to the underground train platforms. My mind was busy digesting the activities of the day, as well as the unfamiliar transportation route. The flow of the crowd was unmistakable, all with their own agendas, all with an autonomous focus, all moving in virtual unison toward the Circle Line train.

Shortly after beginning my descent down the multi-story escalator, a sound broke through the stale drone of the rush-hour flow. Still a long distance away, I saw a young man, guitar in hand, standing at the very base of the grand escalator. With skill his fingers moved across the strings, his left hand finding the chords, his right hand plucking and strumming in appropriate variance.

Even without electronic reinforcement, the music exploded from the instrument. One guitar, yet the sound filled the entire area with sweet refreshment, for this young man had discovered something special. In that one particular spot in the station, the acoustics rivaled those in London's finest theaters. This litter-strewn, graffiti-laced transportation center had offered him an opportunity, and he had seized it.

Perhaps you're not on the stage of your choice. Perhaps you wish there were more spotlights or grander surroundings. My suggestion is simple. Instead of concerning yourself with the auditorium, find a place where the acoustics are great. A place where the work of your hands has a chance to resonate through the lives of others. A place where the joy of playing becomes a reward in itself. A place where those who experience your work will be touched by the result, as well as the effort.

Many are those who moan about the size and location of the stage, but a wise few find a place where the acoustics are great, and without artificial reinforcement, they give us their best. How do we know them? They are a clean fresh breeze through the musty mediocrity. They are unmistakable.

Play where the acoustics are best and let somebody else worry about the size of the stage.

Have a great week.

Walls That Wobble

As part of my basement-remodeling project, I've constructed a shower. Two of the three walls around the shower area required routine wall construction, but the third presented a unique opportunity. Because the ceilings in my basement are very high, I decided to create a wall that only reached part way to the supporting ceiling joists above. This would make the room feel less confined.

Once the rough construction was complete, I was faced with a problem. The wall's abbreviated height was esthetically pleasing, but because it was connected to solid surfaces on only two of the four sides, it wobbled. I did my best to come up with a way to strengthen and stabilize the wall, but with little success.

Then, my friend Mark and his family arrived from San Diego for a visit. Along with being one of the finest men I know, Mark is a structural engineer. It occurred to me that Mark might be able to solve my wobbly wall problem, and soon we were downstairs tugging, evaluating, and analyzing.

Mark quickly understood what I was trying to accomplish and why my problem existed. He then proceeded to give me three or four options to try. All of his suggestions left the design the same, while providing considerable focus on the connection to the lone vertical wall that I could tie into.

Several days after we'd said good-bye to our friends, I wrapped my tool belt around my waist and headed downstairs to implement Mark's suggestions. When the improvements were complete, I was thrilled to note that nearly all of the play and movement were gone.

While I am thankful to Mark for his expert structural advice, I am more thankful for the stability and strength that his friendship provides. Mark knows my weaknesses. He knows the areas of my life that are wobbly. Over the years, his encouragement, example, and discipline have helped to anchor and strengthen the exposed corners of my personal life. He's asked the tough questions, probed the right areas, and provided meaningful suggestions.

Good friends make us stronger. They understand who we want to be, and give us support and accountability to be just that. Do you have a wall that wobbles? Find a good friend, a structural engineer of a friend, and take some solid advice.

Thanks Mark. It worked, in more ways than one.

Have a great week.

Say "Yes" to the Mud

Greetings to you this Monday morning.

Our plans for the weekend included a family hike, but the consistent drizzle put those plans in jeopardy. When Sunday afternoon came, the rain mercifully relented so we bundled up for our march to and ascent up a nearby hill. The first bit of our trip was on paved sidewalks, but soon we came to a field we would have to cross. As we began our trek forward, it became obvious that although the rain had stopped, the ground was still in bad shape. With each step, the mud oozed up around our hiking boots, firmly attaching itself. Each step brought a new layer of mud and additional weight.

For the most part I hate mud. I enjoy watching others play games in it, but personally I dislike it. Consequently, I have trained my children in the proper avoidance techniques. Typically when we walk, I stay in front warning of problem areas. I've been known to chastise the children for careless contact with the sticky substance. That is why when we found ourselves surrounded by mud, I faced a parental dilemma. With few options, we pressed on.

By the time we'd completed our journey across the field, our boots were hopelessly caked with gooey mud. So much so that the situation became humorous. As we trudged onward, some areas we crossed knocked off muddy layers, while others added to the woeful condition of our boots. Finally we reached the top. While I was marveling at the view, Erik interrupted. "Dad," he said with tender sincerity, "thanks for letting us walk through the mud." I could hardly believe it! Here we were at the summit and Erik was still pondering with astonishment the fact that I'd surrendered to my enemy—mud.

As he wandered off to explore, I stood for a moment in introspection. For once I'd said yes to the mud, ignoring the obvious and immediate obstacles in favor of the overall objective, a wonderful hike. For once I'd bitten my tongue about the pathway in order to give approval to the journey.

"Thanks for letting us walk through the mud." I won't soon forget that look or that line. Sometimes it's best to say yes to the mud.

Have a great week.

Turbulence

Greetings to you
this Monday morning.

My flight from Amsterdam to Detroit was scheduled to take just over seven and a half hours. It was a routine so familiar that I have the flight details memorized. Once airborne, the flight attendants come through the aisles with beverage service and nuts. Roughly forty-five minutes later it's time for lunch, then coffee and cleanup. Generally, I have enough time prior to the start of lunch to get some work done. I read a few memos, type a few notes on my laptop, or digest a few articles that one person or another has given me to read. Last week was no exception.

Before my lap-tray became designated for culinary purposes, I had made a substantial dent in the work I had with me. I made a mental commitment to finish it off as soon as lunch was finished. Instead, I was overcome with a very strong urge to nap. I tucked my laptop away, stowed my papers in their proper pouch in my briefcase, and reclined my seat as far as it would go. Moments later I was lulled to sleep by the whine of the powerful jet engines.

I'm not sure how long I had been sleeping when I was suddenly jostled awake by unexpected turbulence. Within a few seconds the "Fasten Seat Belt" sign was illuminated with the accompanying chime, and the lead flight attendant came through to make sure everyone was complying.

A quick glance out the window beside me showed perfectly clear skies, but that 747 continued to pitch and shake. I made several more attempts to drift back to sleep, but to no avail. By the time we reentered stable air, I was wide awake and returned to the work I'd promised to complete.

As a general rule, turbulence is something I'd just as soon avoid. It's unsettling and uncomfortable. For the most part, I prefer a smooth road and predictable results. Yet, over time, I've learned that when the travel is calm it is far too easy to drift off, to lose concentration, to forget what's important. Turbulence can serve as a useful wake-up call.

By the time flight sixty-seven touched down in Detroit, I had finished my tasks. Don't begrudge a bump or two along the way if it wakes you to the important things in life.

Have a great week.

Invite Defeat

Greetings to you
this Monday morning.

Over the past several years, my family and I have had the privilege of getting to know a fine young man who has become one of our favorite visitors. When Aaron comes over we often play ping pong together. He plays the game exceptionally well.

Last Monday night, shortly after we'd finished dinner, the phone rang and it was Aaron wondering if I'd be interested in a friendly game or two. Roughly an hour later, we were in the basement knocking a small white ball back and forth with all the skill we could muster. Playing this sport with Aaron makes this friendly little game a physical workout. By the end of the evening, I was hot and tired.

On this particular evening, Aaron played exceptionally well. He easily took the first three games. Game four seemed to be a turning point for my game. I took that one and the next two, knotting the evening series at three games apiece. But in game seven, Aaron returned to the winning form he had displayed earlier and I ended up on the short end. After Aaron left for home, I mentioned to my son Andrew that I had pushed Aaron to seven games. He knows Aaron's reputation as a ping pong player, and of course, he knows me by more than reputation. After a moments pause, and the appropriate level of surprise, Andrew looked at me and asked, "Dad, do you really think Aaron was playing his hardest when he played you?" Andrew didn't mean any disrespect, he sincerely wondered, and in the moments that followed, so did I. Had games four through six simply been a gift?

I'll never know if Aaron played his best that night, but I do know that he made me play mine. He made me hustle more, think more, execute better, plan ahead, and react more quickly. I like winning, but I also know that if I'm going to improve my game, I have to play people like Aaron. People who push me, challenge me, exploit my weaknesses, and test my strengths. I need people who are better than I am to make me more like I want to be.

Don't restrict your competition to those you can beat. Invite defeat. It's the only way to make improvements in the things you want to do better.

Have a great week.

Safe Places

I t was reminiscent of a giant Fourth of July show—the flashes, the booms, the anticipation of the grand finale. The difference was that this was 2:00 in the morning, and the sound and light show was accompanied by a driving rain and a relentless wind that drove the precipitation sideways, pounding it against the side of the house.

At first the sounds were distant and non-threatening. But, with each passing minute, the lightening grew more intense and the thunder more abrupt and imposing. After a few sizable thunderous reports, I heard a noise at our bedroom door and Alli, our nine-year-old daughter, emerged through the opening. The silhouette of my unnerved child now stood a few feet from the door, amidst the strobe lights and bass drum of the meteorological rock concert. Softly she whispered, "I'm scared," and without a word, Mary lifted the covers in invitation. No words needed to be spoken. Alli simple slid into position beside her mother. I heard a sigh of relief and soon the breathing pattern of a sleeping child.

The next morning, as I began my fifteen-mile journey to the office, I saw all around me the evidence of the early morning event. Like the litter left after a giant outdoor concert, the streets were strewn with refuse from the undaunted storm. Refuse in the form of branches mostly. Branches that only yesterday clung to strong and sturdy trunks.

I was reminded that at the peak of the storm, a tender spring branch had appeared at my bedroom door, needing reassurance that she would not be torn from the trunk. She needed to know, that no matter how the winds howled or the thunder rolled or the lightening flashed, our grip would remain firm and sure. She needed to be reminded that in spite of the power and pull of a tumultuous day, we would cling to her with uncompromising resolve. It took only minutes, but reassurance came, and with it, confident rest.

Where are the places of safety and assurance in your life? The places to cling? The places of deep and abiding love? The storms will blow, the thunder clap, and the lightening flash. Cling tightly.

Have a great week.

Cricket

Several years ago, we had an opportunity to live in England for six months. Shortly after we arrived I picked up a London newspaper and soon found my way to the sports section. I quickly read the articles about rugby, football (soccer), golf, and tennis, all of which I could follow with some level of general understanding. However, on one of the pages, there was an article covering an international cricket match.

I did my best to read through the article, but soon concluded that I simply didn't know enough about the sport to follow what the author was saying. The unique terms and unfamiliar expressions were baffling and amusing. It just seemed like the game was too slow and too complex to warrant any further attention.

Several weeks later, a business colleague offered me tickets for a county cricket match in nearby Canterbury. After some of my local friends ooed and awed at such an opportunity, I determined that we should at least check it out.

When we arrived on Saturday morning, we learned that the match had begun on Thursday and was not scheduled to end until Monday. The scoreboard was indecipherable. The only thing we could make out was that the home team from Kent County was presently behind 295 to 0. But not to worry, they hadn't started batting yet.

While Mary and Alli read the books they had brought along, Andrew, Erik, and I did our best to understand the game. Every so often I would make my way to the nearest usher to ask questions. Slowly, we began to get a grasp on what was going on. We continued to ask embarrassing questions and listen to the chat around us. Soon, terms like *wicket, pitch* (the English term for *field), over, declare, boundary, maiden, bowl, spinner, seamer, bowler, wicket keeper,* and *silly-point* all began to make sense.

It's easy to scoff at and disregard what we don't understand and haven't explored. Knowledge illuminates, exposes, endears. Insight changes a cynic into a fan, a skeptic into a participant.

The next week, I picked up a copy of the *London Telegraph,* and the boys and I divided the sections among us. A few minutes later, Andrew announced, "Hey Dad, Kent beat Sussex by ten wickets on Friday," and amazingly enough, I was delighted.

Have a great week.

Diverted

Greetings to you
this Monday morning.

The metal barricade in front of us was able to restrain our bodies, but our hearts could not be held back. It had been a full eleven days since we'd last seen Andrew, and all of us were delighted to meet him at Heathrow Airport in London, even at 6:30 in the morning. In front of us were three massive arrival information boards with letters that flipped into position.

When we arrived at the airport, the message board revealed that Andrew's flight would be delayed. Foggy weather had forced a change in the anticipated arrival time to 7:10 A.M. Now we stood in front of a large analog clock counting down the minutes. We learned that once a flight lands, the board would change from "Scheduled at 7:10" to "Landed at 7:10." We watched for just such an announcement. The clock moved past the scheduled time, and we continued to wait.

Twenty minutes later, the letters began to ripple new information before our waiting eyes. We watched with anticipation and then with disappointment as the letters flipped from *Scheduled* to *Diverted*. Soon, next to the word *Diverted* appeared the word *Cardiff*, the city in Wales where Andrew's flight was now headed.

Diverted. That single eight-letter word had completely dashed our hopes. That one verb had slapped our plans for the day in the chops and left us with many more questions than answers. Yet, at 11:10 A.M., we watched as the letters fluttered again and *Scheduled* changed to *Landed*. This time the letters didn't disappoint. Four hours before, the word *diverted* seemed to mean defeat. Now, it was simply an inconvenience.

Seldom do things go exactly as we'd like them to. Sometimes when London is in the plan, Wales is the reality. I've never been to Cardiff. It's only about 125 miles from London. Cardiff is like that disappointment that hits right before you get where you really want to go. It's that place where you begin to question your goal. Don't unload in Wales; stay on the runway, nose pointed to London, and soon the fog will lift. Diverted but not defeated.

Have a great week.

Daddy's Gift

With the remnants of a successful Christmas morning scattered about us, it was time for one last gift. Over the past several years, after all of the traditional gifts have been opened, I pull out one more thing, one last memento for each family member, something we call "Daddy's gifts."

So, about 10:00 A.M. on the twenty-fifth of December, it was "Daddy's gift time." I watched carefully as Alli, my nine-year-old daughter, opened her gift. In a long, slender necktie box, I had placed an envelope containing a gift certificate entitling her to spend fifteen dollars at Dana's Boutique. Alli has purchased many gifts at Dana's Boutique, primarily for her friends who have pierced ears. Alli does not have pierced ears, but Dana's also sells a wide variety of other things that could catch a young girl's fancy. Alli simply looked at me with thoughtful eyes and said thanks. Then, with a surprise lump in my throat I asked, "Would you like to get your ears pierced?" Alli's look of shock and absolute delight said it all.

For the last two years I'd succeeded in brushing the question aside by simply saying no without extended discussion. That was a father's prerogative, I reasoned. But, for some reason, this Christmas seemed like the right time. So, wrapped in the camouflage of a tie box, I gave Alli more than a fifteen dollar gift. I gave her permission.

In that moment, and not until that moment, I realized that I'd said yes to my little girl's plea to start the process of becoming a young lady. I said yes to letting her feel pain, to letting her assume responsibility, to letting her grow up. In that instant, I realized that one chapter had closed and another had begun—all because Daddy had given permission. Permission to do it differently. Maybe even permission to fail, but definitely permission to take responsibility. Her consequences, her ears.

The following morning at Dana's, I stood in front of my little Alli and watched as someone I'd never seen before pierced those two precious ears. I'd said yes. I'd given permission. Permission is something we give or withhold each and every day—to family, to friends, to coworkers. Permission to do it differently. Permission to take responsibility. Permission to grow.

Have a great week.

Determination

The thud and rattle I heard from Andrew's upstairs bedroom sent those parental juices of frustration and irritation rushing through my veins. It was late, I was cold and wet, and it was most certainly time for the kids to be in bed.

We'd just returned from two baseball games in a steady drizzle. Andrew's eighth-grade team had prevailed in two lopsided efforts, pushing their league record to four wins and no losses. By all accounts, it wasn't a bad way for a fourteen-year-old to spend a Saturday evening. But Andrew's mood was more somber. With fifteen aspiring young men on his team, playing time has been hard to come by. Even with two wins in which his team outscored the opponent 35 to 6, Andrew's only appearance came in the last inning of the last game.

As I began to make my way up the stairs to express my feelings about the noise level, the realization of what I was hearing hit me full force. The noise I heard was a familiar one—the sound of Andrew's weights. Weights that he'd begun lifting nearly six months before in preparation for his upcoming baseball season. Weights that Andrew believed would make him stronger, more confident, and better able to contribute to the success of the Coca-Cola™ Reds. Weights of determination and drive.

I'm afraid I would have been sulking. I'm afraid I would have been making excuses or pointing a finger of blame. I'm afraid I would have gone to bed believing "it's not fair." Yet, buried in the heart of this kid was the belief that someday his chance will come, and when it does, he wants to be ready. Today's disappointment is converted to determination and with it the commitment to prepare.

How about the team you're on? Are you playing on the second string? Do you feel overlooked and under-appreciated? That thud and rattle I heard late last Saturday night was the sound of my fourteen-year-old teaching me to be patient, to dig deeper, to work harder, to grow stronger—a lesson about not giving up, a lesson about preparation. You keep lifting those weights, Andrew, for last Saturday night, you hit a home run without even swinging a bat.

Have a great week.

Making the Harmony Work

A wonderful family wedding in Nashville, Tennessee, gave us a great opportunity to reconnect with friends and family that we hadn't seen for some time. The weekend raced by and exceeded my expectations on every front.

At the conclusion of the weekend, we got together for a time to reflect and reminisce. As part of that time, an aunt requested that my siblings and I sing a family favorite. This is a song that we have sung for years. Sunday morning the group was small and my brother Sam and I comprised the entire bass section.

I thoroughly enjoy singing with my family. Although I would never sing a solo, that is not a prerequisite for singing with the group. My brother Sam is much the same way. Although I've never heard him sing a solo, I trust his skill and ability. He's a team member, a group player, a contributor.

What happens when Sam and I sing together is that we lean on each other. Not literally, but almost. As the song progresses and the music gets more complicated, Sam and I, side by side, listen more intently to each other to make certain that we're holding up our part of the harmony. Sam finds a note that I'm uncertain of and I do the same for him. Together we get the job done. Together we carry our share of the load.

There wasn't a question in my mind on Sunday. I needed Sam. He made it possible for me to do what I was asked to do. I did the same for him. Together we were the bass section. Together we helped make the harmony work.

Sunday underscored what is written across my life in many areas. I need people. I need teammates, business associates, friends who are willing to lean my way so that I can more easily find the notes I'm uncertain of. And I know they won't hesitate to lean my way when they are uncertain. Together we fill out the bass section. Part of the whole. Part of the blend.

Teamwork. It's enough to make an observer a participant, enough to make two businessmen a bass section. Lean toward each other. Listen. Then sing your part. Thanks Sam for belting out what I wasn't sure of.

Have a great week.

Passion

Greetings to you
this Monday morning.

The smell greeted me as I walked through the back door of our house. Not just any smell; this one was special. It was a compelling invitation to the kitchen table. Mary was hard at work in front of the stove keeping the various dishes moving at the same pace. The oven, stove, and electric frying pan were all being used for the purpose at hand.

Ironically, this was the first home-cooked meal I had enjoyed in several days. I had been on the road visiting with individuals at a couple of very successful companies. I had listened intently throughout the course of the week as each one told me the true story behind his or her success. I had been privy to the vision, mission, and strategies that had converted ideas, some scratched out on restaurant napkins, into publicly traded stock. I heard key leaders in these organizations describe what they believed uniquely qualified their companies as excellent.

As I listened, a single underlying characteristic possessed by each of these individuals kept creeping into my consciousness—*passion*. These individuals believed in their businesses. They believed that the market needed what they were selling. They believed that although competition existed, they had something special to offer.

Now, as I made my way into our kitchen to enjoy the meal my wife had so carefully prepared, something occurred to me. What made the organizations I had just visited so inviting was that their passion for their product or service created an aroma that burst boldly out of the front door of their operations. Each group had used care to select the proper ingredients for success, but it was passion that warmed them into a meal. It was that meal that created an undeniably attractive smell. And it was the smell that made for a compelling invitation to enjoy.

Passion is what turns a recipe into a feast and brings out the very best in the ingredients. Without passion, there is no compelling aroma, no enticing scent. With it, the moment a door is open, the story is out.

Have a great week.

The Grand View

Greetings to you
this Monday morning.

I grew up in a suburb roughly thirty miles west of Chicago, yet it wasn't until a flight this past weekend that I gained a true perspective of the Windy City.

My travel plans were to fly to Oslo, Norway, out of Kansas City with a stop in Detroit. As the plane lifted off, it was evident that the afternoon views would be unrestricted. I wasn't quite sure where our flight pattern would take us, but the captain had informed us that we would be cruising at 33,000 feet. At one point I looked up and my eye caught sight of the edge of a large body of water. I quickly surmised that we were approaching Lake Michigan. Moments later, I traced the shoreline both north and south until I caught a glimpse of what I had been hoping to see. Chicago.

At 33,000 feet, the standard Chicago landmarks were still visible—the towering buildings, the outlying airports, the airstrip along the lakeshore, the major concrete arteries leading in all directions. I knew what I was looking at, but for the first time, I could see the context in which the city exists. I could see the accumulation of steel and concrete that characterizes downtown. And I could also see far enough north to where the land once again reverts to quiet farmland and far enough south to capture the curve at the bottom of Lake Michigan. For the first time in my life, I could see a place as big as Chicago in context. The grand view took nothing away from my previous perspective. It simply added a framework.

From the streets of Chicago, my perspective is very different. Traffic, congestion, construction, pedestrians, and the size are overwhelming. On Sunday afternoon, while towering 33,000 feet above, it looked quite manageable.

This experience made me think about the challenges and issues in my life right now and how enormous and confusing they appear. I thought about the difficulty of maintaining motivation and creativity in the midst of the challenges and problems that regularly confront me. Then I thought about my view from 33,000 feet. I simply need perspective.

In a traffic jam? Congested, gridlocked, frustrated? Change your view and find a context. It will alter your outlook.

Have a great week.

Dusseldorf

We pulled away from our gate in Munich right on time, an accomplishment I found reassuring as I thought about my two connecting flights. Next stop—Amsterdam, about a ninety-minute flight. After a small breakfast, a short nap, and some reading, my flight began its final descent. But there was a problem. As we continued downward, the visibility worsened. Then, unexpectedly, the pilot of the aircraft powered the 737 engines into full thrust, and we instantly began to climb. Moments later the pilot reported that ground visibility was too poor to attempt a landing. We would circle for a time, hoping that conditions would improve.

An hour later, the pilot reported that we were being re-routed to Dusseldorf Airport in northern Germany. Parked on the ground in Dusseldorf, the minutes melted away. When the time for my connecting flight to Detroit had passed, I found a flight schedule book on the plane and discovered that the last connecting flight from Amsterdam to Detroit would be leaving in just over three hours. Finally, we were told that we would be boarding a shuttle bus to the terminal where another bus would take us on to Amsterdam. This would take approximately three additional hours.

As soon as we arrived in the terminal, I found a phone and contacted a travel agent. After explaining my dilemma, I waited on hold while she researched my problem. With each passing moment, I found myself increasingly anxious, thinking about the plans I would have to cancel, the calls I would have to make, the people I would disappoint. Then, the silence was broken by the words I wanted to hear. A flight was scheduled to leave Dusseldorf in one hour for JFK Airport in New York. Once in New York, I would take a cab to LaGuardia Airport for a connecting flight to Kansas City. If all went well, I would be home by 10:00 P.M.

Sometimes, the route from Munich to Kansas leads through Dusseldorf. Sometimes Amsterdam gets fogged in. Sometimes, our best laid plans fade away as we circle the airport, waiting for our options to improve.

Hold on to your goals, and don't be discouraged if you're rerouted to Dusseldorf along the way. You can still make Kansas before the day is done.

Have a great week.

Managing the Moments

Greetings to you
this Monday morning.

Since moving to Kansas more than four years ago, the "Tour de Shawnee" bike tour has become a favorite annual happening for us.

Each participant has the option of three different courses. The length of the journey is the prime variable in each. The shortest was ten miles, the middle distance was twenty-five miles, and the serious trip went fifty miles. The boys and I have always opted for the middle distance.

On our first year of riding, we woke to a perfect morning—cool, no breeze, and bright sunshine, all adding to the false hope that the ride would glide by like a Sunday stroll in the park. About two miles into the ride, we were introduced to the rolling Kansas countryside. The first few hills passed without much effort. Up and down we rode, relishing the downside, grinding through the up.

At one point, we climbed to the top of a rise, only to get a perfect view of the hills ahead. I was riding with Erik, my youngest son, and we both groaned as we began our descent with the view of the pending hills just ahead. This rapid roll down the hill had lost its luster knowing that there were substantial climbs to come. I encouraged Erik to look at the hills one at a time. Then, to break each hill down into smaller sections, i.e., "to that tree" or "up to that post," finding accomplishment in the small steps rather than being overwhelmed with the big picture. It was that perspective that carried us through the twenty-five-mile course.

Life has a similar terrain. We live for the coast down, only to find that the climb back up is overwhelming. As we look ahead we tend to be overcome with concerns about tomorrow and beyond, and as a result we miss the thrill of rising to the top of today's crest. In the meantime, we fail to learn that each day that we grow and move forward we have accomplished something significant. The worry about tomorrow's hills often robs us of the delight in accomplishing today's mission.

Break those big, impossible journey's in your life into small manageable moments. Look for the trees or fence posts along the way that show that you're making progress. Then savor each accomplishment.

Have a great week.

First on the Scene

Greetings to you
this Monday morning.

As I made my way out of the double doors at the front of the high school, I noticed a group of about ten boys playing what appeared to be a makeshift game of keep-away with a hard rubber football. The group ranged in age from about five to fourteen.

Now, just a few feet from the group, I witnessed a pass that landed in the middle of the group. A scramble ensued, which I could hear as I kept my focus forward. Moments later, I felt a sharp pain on the right side of my face. I reached up to make sure my contacts were still in place, and then I realized I had been hit by an errant pass. I quickly turned and panned the hushed group.

It didn't take long for my eyes to meet those of a young boy, about seven years old, who apparently had thrown the pass. Amazingly, he didn't try to escape or pass the blame. Instead, in full non-verbal confession, he stood sobbing, looking square at me, his hapless, unsuspecting adult target.

Whatever my first reaction had been, all my attention was now focused on this incredibly regretful boy. I set my things down and rapidly made my way to him. It was obvious that he was feeling more pain than I was. I put my arm around him, and through thick, earnest tears, he choked out the words, "I'm sorry." No denial, no justification, no shift of blame, no attempt to soften the responsibility, just "I'm sorry" from the depths of his heart.

Why are those two little words so difficult to express? When I make a mistake, I want my errant pass to hurt me as much as it does the person who took it on the side of the face. That is the only way real restoration is possible.

Five minutes later, as I hurried back to the school with another load of things from the van, I caught this young boy's eyes again. Immediately they flooded with tears once again. This time I put my arm around him, looked him in the eye and said with full sincerity, "I've forgiven you," and I had.

The next time I hurt someone, I want my tears to be the first on the scene. No justification or rationalization. Just honest regret. It's the only way to turn errant passes into touchdowns.

Have a great week.

Enjoy the Process

It seems that word is out, Erik loves jigsaw puzzles. From conventional to three dimensional, Erik loves them all.

In the past few years, I've observed firsthand the skillful approach he takes to these puzzles. With a picture of the finished product close by, he carefully organizes each piece into its appropriate category. Edge pieces in one spot, certain distinctly colored pieces in another. One-bump shapes here, two-bump shapes over there.

Then, he begins to put the pieces together. First the edge, then a slow migration inward. Each newly connected piece adding to an evolving picture. Each a celebration. There are no shortcuts, there are no grand slams. Each piece must be carefully fitted to its neighbor, one at a time.

Sometimes the pieces fit in rapid succession, at other times, it seems to be an endless chore to find one missing piece. But, finally, the last piece slides into place, and we marvel once again at the beauty of the accomplishment.

Without exception, the combination of the pieces is brighter and more wonderful than the example he was given to follow. Without exception, the process held its own reward, for within days, the image is dismantled and another goal lies in pieces across the table.

The entire process reminds me a great deal of what organizations and individuals go through from time to time. It's about executing a vision or implementing a mission. A vast array of varied pieces. The naive rush of excitement at the start, followed by hours, days, weeks, and months of patient effort moving slowly toward the objective. The pieces lay scattered across the table. A disjointed image of unrelated events that will somehow fit together to form a finished picture. I have goals. I have personal and professional objectives. All of those pieces are in front of me now. Disconnected, upside down, but there. There are no shortcuts. The pieces fit one at a time. Some come together with surprising ease, others are painful to find and confusing to place.

Be patient; work hard. Enjoy the process as well as the prospect. Keep checking the image of the finished product. The hard work has the potential to produce a portrait that surpasses any picture you might have imagined. Then, once complete, find a new picture. Another goal. An expanded vision.

Have a great week.

The Track

A s I boarded the train for the trip from Paris to southern England by way of the Channel Tunnel, I was fascinated by the sleek appearance of the rail cars. Each was bright yellow and white in a stylish and impressive mix. The train engine was an aerodynamically contoured marvel, designed to cut through the wind with peak efficiency. The interior was constructed for comfort and class.

Shortly after we were seated, the train pulled away from the Gare Du Nord station in Paris with amazing ease. Moments later we were on our way toward the French countryside with increasing velocity. Within twenty minutes of departure, we were informed that the train had reached its peak traveling speed of 186 miles per hour. We were now blistering through the landscape at remarkable speeds, yet experiencing a completely smooth ride. There was no jerking or jostling about, just the consistent drone of the powerful engine tugging us toward our final destination.

While it is the wonderfully stylish train that adorns the promotional photographs, it is the perfectly constructed track that deserves most of the credit for the incredible ride. The track determines the destination; the track determines the quality of the ride; the track supports the movement above. It is the track that makes the difference.

A premium is placed on speed and style. We want to get there quicker, and we want to look good on the way. We want to move ahead, fast. Yet, the focus of our attention should really be on the track on which we run. A track constructed with the goals we set and the plans we make. The very things that ensure that when we move, we're moving in the right direction, and with as smooth a ride as possible.

When you take the time to lay the track and make certain that you're moving in the proper direction, then the journey becomes a celebration of realized plans and goals accomplished.

We all dream of going 186 miles per hour. Just take the time to make sure the track is firmly laid and leads you toward your final destination. You might even find that with the proper planning, even an obstacle as imposing as the English Channel is just part of the journey.

Have a great week.

I Saw It in Enfield

One of the things that was a substantial surprise to us in the months that we lived in Europe was the minimal variation in weather. Regularly we would get reports from home showing a wide spectrum of temperatures and conditions, but not so in England. The temperatures typically hang close to freezing at night, and slowly moderate during the day. From February through April, the top end of the temperature ranges from forty-five to fifty degrees.

Back in the States, my hope for spring often rested in brief periods of warmer weather. These were premature and temporary, but encouraging. While in the UK, however, the slow incremental change afforded no such optimistic opportunity. Often we were left wondering if spring would ever come.

On one April weekend in England, we visited the small London suburb of Enfield. It was there that I got my answer about spring's arrival. While walking through the center of town, we entered a park area. Evening was beginning to fall, and the light was a bit muted as we marched between the hedgerow into the full park expanse. There, before me, in the midst of the leafless trees and the dormant grass was a brilliant carpet of color. As though stroked with an artist's brush, there was a mix of purple, yellow, and white. It stretched from corner to corner, emerging right from the lawn itself.

As had been the case everyday since we arrived, we were attired in our winter coats. Collars up, gloves on, defending us against the crisp English air. To us it felt much as it had in late January when we arrived. But with one breathtaking sight, spring had announced its arrival. With determination and defiance the spring crocuses had attacked the firm grip of winter and proclaimed it vulnerable. With an army of color, they had invaded the drab remains and pronounced it conquerable. Hope had bloomed during the final watch of winter, while I was still a prisoner of the lifelessness.

Bloom. Bloom when it's gray. Bloom while winter is still on the throne. Bloom while most are still held within the solid grasp of winter. Proclaim it conquerable. Splash hope across the canvas of doubt.

It's Monday, the air is crisp, the trees bare, the grass dormant, but today I know that spring is on the way. I saw it myself in Enfield.

Have a great week.

The Word is *Green*

During our stay in England, Mary, the kids, and I boarded a train one Saturday bound for Oxford, a lovely city known for learning and wisdom. What I hadn't realized before was that Oxford University consists of thirty-nine colleges that lie in close proximity to the city itself. The colleges themselves are autonomous and focus on different areas of study and learning. Of particular note to me was All Souls College, located in the oldest part of the city.

This institution has a total student body of seventy-two. Each student is granted a lifetime fellowship. Given these facts, it's not surprising that the entrance process is rigorous and highly contested. Our guide explained that multiple tests are administered to each aspiring All Souls applicant. There are many written tests, some oral, and finally the grand finale in the form of a grueling essay exam.

The essay exam is itself a three-hour ordeal. Once seated, the test taker is given a single word upon which he or she must be prepared to expound with significance for 180 minutes. Last year's word was *green.* Now let me say that I would barely be able to elicit 180 seconds worth of thoughtful response on the subject of *green,* let alone sixty times that.

For the balance of the day, I couldn't help thinking about that All Souls challenge. There was so much at stake, so much riding on that simple word. Perhaps words in previous years were more inspiring, with multiple possibilities. But *green?* Then slowly, in small increments, my thoughts began to germinate and the ideas began to flow. I felt challenged to explore, stretch, and expand. I quickly realized that somewhere, just beyond the veneer of immediate thought, there are wonderfully creative concepts waiting for the light of day.

I will never seek to enroll at All Souls College, but I learned a lesson there nonetheless. For if a wise and practiced mind can make three hours of sense out of the word *green,* how much easier it ought to be to creatively apply myself to the challenges of my own life. Resist the urge to find the easy answers. Challenge your mind to stretch and grow. Even a word like *green* begins to explode when you take the time to explore.

Have a great week.

Engineering Work

Our time in England often included weekends spent exploring the local countryside. We used the British rail system for most of our travels, and each week, I would dutifully pick up the necessary fliers indicating the weekend departure and arrival times.

On one particular weekend upon arrival at the Folkestone Central rail station, we were notified that our train would not be running to the London terminal shown on our schedule. Instead we would be routed to another within the city. The change simply meant that we would have to change our routing on the Underground. Once at Cannon Street Station in London, we noticed several messages on an information board that informed us of changes in the subway routing for the weekend. Once again our plans would have to change in order to make it to the Kings Cross station that would be our departure terminal for our journey to Cambridge. All in all our travel took about an hour longer than we had planned.

In each case, the same reason was given for the changes. Engineering work. The weekend is dedicated to this purpose, allowing orange-vested workers time to tighten, replace, adjust, reinforce, and inspect. A time without traffic, without interruption. Inconvenient but necessary.

The demands of daily living often take a toll on our lives. A toll that stresses the rails, that wears the switches, that shifts the ground. A toll that left unchecked begins to show itself in the quality of the ride, in reliability, and the attitude of those on the journey.

I noticed another sign at the terminal in Cambridge. It was a sign indicating that 98.2 percent of arrivals and departures are on time. A proudly displayed sign that is the direct result of a specific weekend activity—engineering work.

Are you noticing that the ride is rougher than it used to be? Are you letting things slip that used to be second nature? Maybe it's time to post the sign, slip into the bright-orange vest, and plan an interruption in your regular schedule. A time without traffic, without interruption, and without a load. A time to tighten, replace, adjust, reinforce, and inspect. A time for engineering work.

Have a great week.

The Rock Pile

Greetings to you
this Monday morning.

This past weekend, we all piled in the van and drove to a small town in the vicinity looking for a place to explore. We climbed a hill close to where we had parked and walked toward a quietly rolling field, where we spotted a hill emerging in one corner. At the base of the hill there was an area of exposed chalk rock that proved to be an invitation for fun.

A few minutes of exploration proved adequate for Mary and Alli, but the boys and I had just begun. The soft crumbly chalk rock lay in piles at the base of the hill, providing all we needed for a friendly game of target practice. Standing about thirty to forty feet away from the wall of exposed rock, we took turns aiming, winding up, and then hurling a rock in the direction of a predetermined target. We kept no score and offered no prizes, but still we hurled away. Sometimes on target, more often not. Our reward? Laughter and congratulations. We had found our game. Common ground. No batteries required.

By the time we finally tired of the game, Mary and Alli had walked all the way across the next field. As we made our way toward them, I thought about what had just happened. As a forty-year-old, I can seem hopelessly middle-aged to two teenaged boys. Our thoughts and priorities move in completely different directions. Seldom do those paths get close, let alone meet. Yet, as I looked down at my chalk-whitened hands, I realized that the lines had crossed. The intersection point was at a pile of chalk rocks at the edge of an open field. The complexities of the parent/teenager relationship brought together at a rock pile.

When relationships seem complicated and distant, when common ground is shrinking, when the prospects for compromise are fading, meet at a place of simple agreement. Meet at the rock pile. No pretense. No politics. No preaching.

Whether it's a teenager, a parent, a neighbor, or a coworker, the first step toward resolving difficult issues is often meeting at the rock pile. A place of shared resources. A place of common ground. A place with a mutual target. A place of laughter and congratulations. It works.

Have a great week.

A Vaccination for Life

This past January in preparation for our pending trip to Europe, Mary took the kids to the pediatrician for an update on vaccinations. It seems strangely illogical that a small dose of a germ willfully and knowingly placed into the body can actually create a resistance to disease in the future. Yet, that is exactly what happens. The life-threatening epidemics of yesterday are easily managed by a dose of the sickness today.

So, one by one, Andrew, Erik, and Alli all took their shots one more time—enduring the small stick and the short duration of feeling mediocre afterwards, for the prospect of never having to face the diseases of yesterday.

What none of us realized when we left the United States was that three and a half months later, while still in Europe, another vaccination was in store. This one, however, didn't occur in the doctor's office. This one didn't involve a stick from a needle, although the impact was every bit as abrupt and shocking. This one didn't create a medical immunity, yet the results will be as far reaching.

This past weekend, while on our way to Munich, we stopped in a typical little Bavarian Village—a quiet, quaint spot that time will never forget. The German people have made certain of that. The place is Dachau, and the images are unforgettable—a portrait of hatred and evil, of pain, isolation, injustice, and suffering. Here, where more than 200,000 prisoners lived and died between 1933 and 1945, the country has erected a graphic memorial raging against the atrocities that marked the Nazi concentration camps. In this place, which marks one of the darkest hours of human existence, a light now shines. Skillfully etched in marble in five languages is the simple inscription: "Never again."

For three young impressionable minds from Kansas this was a vaccination of lifetime proportions. A small dose of the hatred of which man is capable. An abrupt injection of evil. A bitter taste of history for the express purpose of creating the knowledge, understanding, passion, and courage to identify and resist any such terror in the future.

There's another inscription at Dachau. It says this: "Those who forget the past are condemned to repeat it." Visiting Dachau was a vaccination against just such a risk.

Have a great week.

Peggy Brown

Greetings to you
this Monday morning.

Last weekend, we once again took in the sights and sounds of the Kansas City Plaza Art Fair. We had a wonderful time meandering down the blocked-off streets, peering into each booth as we passed. While the event is billed as an art sale, it is more accurately an art museum with price tags. Well-known and correspondingly well-rewarded artists from all over the country set up their displays in an effort to showcase their latest works. We were exposed to everything from jewelry to stick furniture, from still-life to comic strips, from metal work to marble work, all with the flare that makes them unique and intriguing.

As we made our way through the crowd, Mary suddenly announced, "Look, over there, it's Peggy Brown!" I knew immediately that she wasn't referring to an individual named Peggy Brown but rather a booth full of watercolor paintings by an artist named Peggy Brown. We first became familiar with this artist seventeen years before in Fort Wayne, Indiana, and knew her to be a gifted individual who had begun her distinguished career by working from her home while her children were small. Peggy Brown is an artist that Mary and I both enjoy. So much so, that her rendition of a lone tree in the midst of winter now hangs on my office wall. We had not seen her work displayed since we left her studio with our masterpiece in 1978.

Yet it took only an instant for Mary to recognize the unique and unmistakable character of Peggy Brown's watercolor. The art world had certainly recognized it as well. She had the awards, recognition, and price tags to prove it.

What a challenge to consider as we paint on the canvases of our lives—each stroke a reflection of who we are. Each stroke defining our unique and unmistakable character. Just as Peggy Brown's signature graces the right-hand corner of the painting in my office, so too my autograph highlights the work of my hand. Remember that tomorrow's masterpiece depends on the brush strokes of today. Wield your brush with care.

Have a great week.

A Few Simple Words

Greetings to you
this Monday morning.

Last Wednesday, for just the second time this year, I played nine holes of golf. Andrew and Erik joined my father and me for a round at a public course a short distance from home.

As we played, I found myself instructing Andrew after nearly every shot. It seemed to me that his stance wasn't quite right on some shots, his grip on a few more, his alignment on others, and he made a few poor club selections as well. After all, I should know, I had golfed once before this year, and besides I'd spent a good many years on my own learning what sort of things don't work on a golf course. Andrew always listened and did his best to alter whatever it was that I had suggested he alter, obtaining mixed results.

Roughly an hour and a half into the adventure, we found ourselves on the seventh green. Andrew had a six to eight-foot putt to make, and he went through the proper steps in preparation. He had encountered a number of challenging putts during the round, and on each, I had raised my chorus of instruction, but not this time. I decided I'd let him meet the challenge alone. Just as he was beginning to take a few practice swings, my Dad said quite simply and confidently, "Come on Andrew, I know you can do it." Moments later my fourteen-year-old son was stooping over to pull his golf ball out of the cup. He'd done it.

All of my instruction amounted to nothing when compared to those four simple words from his grandpa. We all need to be taught. We all need to know the "hows" of what we are to do, but never underestimate the value of knowing that somebody thinks we "can." Instruction without encouragement leads to a fear of failure. Instruction with encouragement fosters a desire for success. In the one case I spend all my time worrying about missing my goal, in the other I am focused on making it.

Today, someone needs to hear you say, "You can do it." Resist the urge to fix their stance, grip, or club selection, and just let them know you have confidence in them. Success may be just four words away. Say them!

Have a great week.

Carmen

Greetings to you
this Monday morning.

Last Saturday I boarded a flight from Denver to Kansas City. After making my way down the aisle to row 13, I dropped my briefcase on 13D, an aisle seat, and turned to slide in. As I did, I looked squarely into the faces of two elderly women. "We need 13E and 13F," one announced. "Right here," I replied and pointed to the two vacant seats beside mine. Both women lugged carry-on bags, and one clutched a cane.

The first woman looked at me and announced, "We need help," as though she assumed I was an airline employee. Dutifully I responded by loading one bag in the overhead compartment, sliding another under a seat, and carefully placing the cane in a bin behind us. Now, with everyone seated, I responded to 13E's plea for help with her seat belt.

About the time we were being pushed back from the gate, 13E asked, "Do you know where Branson is?" I soon learned that these two travel companions were en-route from San Francisco to Branson, Missouri, with a "Golden-Age" travel club. By this point, I'd noticed a bright red button on 13E's blouse that stated her name was Carmen.

Carmen addressed me many times. Typically her lead line was some variation of, "Can you help me. . . ?" During the flight, I opened a bag of peanuts and retrieved a soft drink from the flight attendant. I answered questions about where to eat dinner in Kansas City, and I gave my solicited opinion on pending weather patterns. I even began to enjoy these interruptions.

I was struck by Carmen's honesty, her ability to ask for help in this day of self-sufficiency and independence. I sat, between requests, wondering how long it had been since I looked squarely into someone's face and said, "I need help!" It's been a long time. Yet I do need help. I need help at work, I need help as a husband, and I need help as a father. I need help sifting through the troublesome issues of life, but I'm afraid that pride often forces me to rely on my own limited resources. What a mistake.

Saturday night, somewhere between Denver and Kansas City, an old woman named Carmen taught me how important it is to be honest enough to ask for help.

Have a great week.

"I'm for the Royals!"

One evening, I found myself in our family minivan with a load of children. Some of them were mine; most of them were not. Trying to be more than a typical voiceless chauffeur, I asked, "Who are you kids for in the World Series?" Immediately I got a flurry of answers.

The young lad seated behind me had remained quiet through my little exercise and therefore, I asked, "Adam, who are you for in the World Series?" Without hesitation, he blurted out, "The Royals." Since the Royals weren't in the Series that year, I conjectured that he had not completely understood the question. So I repeated it, this time naming the two Series contenders. "I said I want the Royals," Adam announced confidently.

I proceeded with a parental explanation that by the end of October, there are only two teams left in major league baseball, and they are playing each other for the championship. It is from those two teams that a favorite must be picked. Adam listened, then thoughtfully replied, "I know all that, but I'm still for the Royals." It didn't seem to bother him that most of the players on his revered home team were now happily vacationing in bass boats or hunting lodges. Adam was for the Royals, period!

Loyalty is a lost virtue. We seem to have lost that deep sense of commitment that transcends losing seasons and unfulfilled expectations. I wish life were always full of championship seasons. I wish the World Series was always a sure thing. But, from time to time, I can barely stay in the game, let alone win it. In those moments and at those times, I want a friend like Adam on my side. I want some-body standing beside me who knows that although I've missed the World Series this year, there's always next year. Not naive, but committed. Not fool-hearty, but devoted.

Loyalty transcends slumps, losing streaks, and single-season records. It stands firm, unmoved by periodic lulls in progress. Loyalty raises its voice when the stands are empty as well as when they're full. It believes, when doubt is more popular. Loyalty cheers for the Royals, even when some other team is in the World Series. Loyalty is the mark of a true fan, but more importantly, a true friend.

Have a great week.

A Winter Shadow

This past weekend, under the brilliance of a bright blue sky, Mary and I went on a long walk through a local park. With our dog Mackie at leash length, we made our way along a pathway that led us through fields and forests.

It was just past noon when I became aware of the lengthy shadow that accompanied our nine-year-old mutt. It stretched about ten feet in front of me. Had we been walking at approximately the same time in the day a few months before, the shadowed image would have been much smaller. But now, with October and November behind us and December at hand, the location of the sun had drastically changed. There was a growing crispness in the air. Winter was preparing to take up dominant residence. And so, as the phenomenon of another passing season unfolds, the resulting affects of sunshine against a solid object become more pronounced.

Many will shrink back from the bite of the winter wind, but there will be others who find the challenges of winter offer a place of determination and strength. These individuals will cast a shadow that is long and unmistakable.

Lesser souls will find solace next to a crackling fire, in denial of winter's grip. They long for the full and easy light of a summer sun. In summer, the shadows of a noon day sun vary little from individual to individual. Their reach is measured in inches not feet. But winter comes, and those with only summer substance retreat.

As the forecast of life changes from balmy to blustery, so too the impact of those who will stand firm. When hope is at its winter solstice, the shadows of those individuals with character extend to great lengths. Lengths that impact and influence. Lengths that encourage and endure. Lengths that help to sustain us until spring comes.

I want to cast a shadow. Not a little, barely noticeable summertime shadow, but a real, dead-of-winter kind of shadow. A shadow that stretches to unimaginable lengths as optimism slips further south. A shadow thrown from a substantial image built with character and integrity. A shadow that demonstrates that there is more to me than seasonal fluff. I want to be solid, sure, and steady. Cast a shadow, and do it in December.

Have a great week.

More Than a Rebound

When the opportunity to play on the eight-grade basketball team presented itself, Andrew hadn't been all that interested. It had been four years since he played competitive ball. There were too many other boys, too many hours of practice, and too many early mornings and late nights. But now, just twelve months later, things had changed. Andrew had grown six inches and added more than forty pounds. These changes sparked a renewed interest in the game. When the ninth-grade team was forming, he got on board.

Friday night, Andrew and his teammates stepped on the court for their first test of the season, and Andrew found himself in the center of the action. Four years before, the only action Andrew had seen was on the perimeter of the playing surface away from all the big guys. But now he was a big guy, and he positioned himself dutifully close to the basket.

As the first eight-minute quarter unfolded, however, something became obvious. Andrew was playing in a highly strategic position, justified by his physical stature, and he was a good match for the individual he was playing against. But Andrew, for all the changes that had taken place, still played like an average-sized kid. Everything had changed except his outlook.

Close to the end of that first quarter, an errant shot caromed off of the rim high into the air. Three boys leaped to establish possession, but inches above the rest, Andrew made first claim. In that moment, he got more than a rebound, more than a basketball. In that moment, he caught a glimpse of the significance of change and retrieved his self-confidence as well as the ball.

The competition tried to convince him that he was too short to play inside, but with that rebound, Andrew's outlook had shot up the six inches that his body had already attained. Without the confidence to implement the change, Andrew was simply an average kid with above-average potential. Now, he was a player.

Don't be content to play an average game with above-average potential. It's time to leap for a rebound, stretching to heights you thought were reserved for the big guys. Chances are, you will get the rebound and with it, the confidence to make a difference for the rest of the game.

Have a great week.

Half As Big

Over the extended Thanksgiving weekend, we made our way back to the Chicago area for time with family. On Thursday, the family gathered at my brother's home, which is located in the very town in which I spent my first eighteen years.

The day was full to the brim with sharing, eating, and a general blend of love and life, but at the end of the day, I still had one favor to ask of my family. I was eager to take a short detour past the house where I had grown up. In the spirit of holiday cheer, they consented, and we made our way toward 103 East Park. On the way, I described the house as I remembered it—the corner of Main and Park, open field across the street to the west, open area behind the house that accommodated a swing-set, as well as baseball and football games, an enormous yard that took hours to cut, especially considering the number of elm trees that edged the outside of the lot.

I was sure that in twenty-plus years things had changed, but I wasn't prepared for how much. As we made the right-hand turn off of Roosevelt Road onto Main, now just a block away, I noticed that a nicely black-topped parking lot sat where the ball field had been and office buildings had been built in the open field across the street. Not a single elm tree had survived the onslaught of Dutch Elm disease, and even the yard didn't seem nearly as imposing as I had remembered. But, what really caught me off guard was how small the house seemed. It was as if time had shaved square footage off of the floor plan.

While the family with whom we had spent the day had grown and was continuing to grow both in number and ever-deepening relationships, the family home that once had held us all, now seemed half as big.

Time never increases the size of the things that we buy. Most typically, they are never bigger than they are the moment we first acquire them. Relationships, on the other hand, have the potential to grow well beyond the parameters that first defined them. Wise investors know that dollars spent on a house will never compare to the investment made in building a family.

Have a great week.

An October Snow

Driving through town this afternoon, I saw a remarkable sight. In every neighborhood, on every street, by homes, offices, schools, and stores, piles of branches had been stacked high at curbside. Literally thousands of downed limbs had been gathered for city collection. Never have I seen such uniform destruction of trees.

The culprit was a storm of significant strength that swept through our area last Tuesday. It began with a crisp northerly breeze and a steady drizzle and ended with eight inches of heavy wet snow—a significant amount at any time in Kansas City, but an historic accumulation for October. Yet, it wasn't the volume of snow that posed the problem for the community hardwoods. It wasn't the wind that accompanied the precipitation that caused branches to break in record numbers. It wasn't even the rate at which the snow collected once the temperature touched the freezing mark. What made this storm so incredibly punishing was the fact that most of the trees had not yet lost their foliage from the summer months. As a result, branches that had been showing off vibrant fall colors became a resting spot for heavy, wet flakes, and as the day wore on, branch after branch succumbed to the weight.

Within twenty-four hours, all but the snow-plowed mounds had melted, revealing a battlefield strewn with the casualties of an early wintry attack. The task of cutting, cleaning, piling, replacing, and restoring was now ahead. In its proper time, last Tuesday's storm would have been of little consequence except for providing a good time for delighted school children. But Tuesday, nature's timing was off, and branches and power lines fell in full surrender.

Are you overloaded, weighted down? Are you overcommitted, cracking under the pressure like a hardwood in a too-early winter snow? What starts out as a northerly breeze and a steady drizzle needs to serve as a warning that tomorrow brings a burden of its own. It is when we carry both the leaves of today and the snowfall of tomorrow that limbs crack and branches break. Winter is coming. Welcome it with strength and confidence, but first drop the leaves of fall.

Have a great week.

For the Sake of the Tulips

When we began to make plans for our five-month adventure in Europe, one goal I formulated was to visit the Netherlands during tulip season. I'll never forget the day that dream bloomed into reality. We pulled into the parking lot of a fabulous park called Keukenhof. This unforgettable spot is approximately twenty miles outside of Amsterdam in the Dutch countryside. Each spring, from the end of March to the end of May, the best the world has to offer in bulbed spring flowers are displayed in full regalia.

For four hours, we walked through the sixty-plus acres of brilliant colors and pristine smells. Over the course of an afternoon, we were treated to a floral fireworks show that I'm certain will remain unrivaled in my lifetime. When we were finally able to drag ourselves away, we traveled along the surrounding rural roads. Nearly each mile we drove revealed fields of bright and brilliant color. Stripes of red, yellow, orange, purple, and variations in-between proved an awesome companion along our journey. After a short time our road turned and progressed along the base of a short but pronounced hill. A hill that we were to discover held back the power and might of the sea.

We parked and climbed the rise to the crest. There, to our amazement, we saw water as far as the eye could see, and at a level that was well above the land from which we had just ascended. We had just discovered one of the famous dikes of the Netherlands. A discovery that put an enormous exclamation point behind the pictorial experience we had just enjoyed.

Here, under our feet was the reason that acres of the world's most beautiful flowers were thriving. Here, under a cloak of spring-greened grass was the restraining power that exposed rich dark soil on one side, while holding at bay the fury of an unrelenting foe. A mound of rock and dirt had liberated captive potential. What was once a swamp was now a farm. What was previously a marshland was now a perfect birthing place for the full impact of spring.

When doubt and fear seem to swamp your hopes and dreams, hold them back. When problems obscure your view of the future, build a dike, reclaim the land. The fragrances and colors of your future may well depend on it.

Have a great week.

No Second Chances

Greetings to you
this Monday morning.

Several weeks ago, I had a truly remarkable cultural experience. On a Wednesday evening, we made our way to the Palace Theater for an unforgettable performance of the show *Les Miserables*.

Halfway through the performance when the curtain dropped for intermission, the only expression that I could utter was "Wow." The staging, the orchestration, the lighting, the singing, and the acting had all been extraordinary. The second half was equally as thrilling.

In total, the performance lasted just over three hours. When it was over, the players came to the foreground in bunches to take their bows until only one actor was left to recognize. As the lead performer made his way from off-stage, the crowd, already clapping in sincere appreciation, rose to its feet in unanimous acknowledgment of the marvelous evening performance.

As I walked from the theater, I thought about how demanding and exhausting it would be to pour oneself into a show like *Les Miserables* night after night. The action unfolds, under revealing stage lights, in front of thousands of intensely observant customers. No retakes. No second chances. Just one shot to make each performance a lasting memory.

For me the script changes each day. Sometimes the stage is home, sometimes the office, sometimes the neighborhood, but each day the curtain does go up on a new performance. Each day an audience assembles as the beneficiaries of my efforts. Each day the curtain drops, bringing finality and conclusion. No retakes, no second chances.

Hours ago the curtain was raised on today. What is yet unknown is the passion of my performance and my reaction to those who labor beside me. For my part, I will attempt to pour myself into each act. Aware that an audience exists, an audience expects, an audience awaits. For my part, I will applaud more—aware that the cast around me waits to see just what I think of their efforts.

Perform with passion. Strive for "Wow." Clap with sincerity. The orchestra is tuning up for the finale. No retakes. No second chances.

Have a great week.

Maintaining Direction

During our family time in England, we went on a family hike to the county of Hampshire, well known for what is called the New Forest, an area plentiful in hiking trails and wildlife.

I had purchased a travel guide that gave us bits of useful and interesting information about the region, and in it, reference was made to ten hiking alternatives with a small map and detailed narrative for each. We opted to start in the small town of Minstead. Once parked, I was directed to the right side of the parking lot to a wooden sign that pointed the way and displayed the word *Footpath*. Easy enough. We progressed along the path until we came to a lane, which displayed no clear marking. At this point, I checked the guidebook and found the following message, "Bear left across a footbridge beside a watersplash ford and follow the quiet lane, keeping right at the junction and pass Fleetwater Farm." What clarity, what direction. I was impressed.

This carried us with success until near the end of the route where we once again needed direction. This time the text in the book read, "Take the unmarked path right onto a wide pathway through woodland. The path may become ill-defined in places, but maintain direction; eventually you will emerge into a clearing with a house and smallholding to your right."

I believe that each member of my family, at various stages along the "unmarked and ill-defined" pathway, believed that we were in fact lost. Ambling through the forested terrain without clear marking was a test. All that prompted me forward was the admonishment to "maintain direction." Ultimately, we did emerge into a clearing. Ultimately we did see a house burst through on our right. Ultimately we got back to the clearly marked wooden signs and unmistakable pathway. It simply took a commitment to maintain our direction through the uncertainty.

Sometimes the path is unmistakably marked. At other times a guidebook is required. Sometimes, the best we get is unmarked and ill-defined, and we may feel the urge to change course, to react, to second guess. It is precisely those times that the best advice is to maintain direction. Soon enough, we will emerge into a clearing and the path will once again be obvious.

Have a great week.

A Real Dog Show

Last week, while enjoying a family vacation in Scotland, we followed a handmade sign pointing us to a local sheepdog trial in the little western town of Kilberry.

The road back to the designated area consisted of fourteen single-lane miles with small passing areas along the way. By the time we arrived, the competition was well underway. A blustery northwesterly wind was blowing off of the Atlantic Ocean with unrelenting force, and rain fell in varied proportions throughout the time we spent observing.

Even under these dismal condition, the dogs emerged one by one from the edge of the spectator area, each marching obediently at the side of its master. A red flag was then waved high in the air approximately a quarter of a mile away, and four adult sheep were released into the open field. On command, the sheepdog, usually a black and white Border Collie, would move quickly toward the sheep. Rather than taking the most direct route, however, they would sweep wide, approaching less intrusively from either side. Once positioned in an ideal location, the dog began working with the uncooperative sheep, which included maneuvering them through gates all along a predefined course.

Amazingly, the dogs seemed to love what they were doing. Often, immediately after completing their task, they would quickly return to the edge of the field, eyes pinned on the opposite side, pleading for another opportunity to guide and conquer. What looked like work and frustration to us was a delight to our four-legged competitors. We were also surprised at the consistent method used by the dogs to bring the sheep through the gates. There was no growling and snarling, no direct confrontation, no display of power and force, no barking. Instead, the highly trained animals circled, directed, pointed, blocked, and generally led in such a way that the sheep felt they were choosing their own paths.

All of us were greatly impressed, but more than that, I was challenged. Challenged to lead by directing, resisting the urge to drive with power, to snarl when opposed, to intimidate when undermined, and opting instead to circle, to come alongside, to motivate. Furthermore, I was challenged to love what I do, and do what I love, whether that job is at home, in my yard, or at my desk—bad weather, uncooperative sheep, and all.

Have a great week.

True Colors

In the weeks that have passed since our trip to Europe, we've gotten our final batch of pictures developed. With great delight, we have flipped through them, reliving many of the wonderful experiences that helped to make the time so memorable.

Included in the set that we just retrieved, were pictures from the vacation week we spent in Scotland. When we mentioned to our European friends that we were planning to travel into Scotland, they let us know that it is a beautiful place and then warned us that most of the time the weather is dismal. After a week in the country, we found that they were right on both counts.

It was while reliving some of the special Scottish experiences, via photographs, that something occurred to me. Of all the many pictures that we took during our six-month adventure, none turned out as well as our pictures of Scotland. In simplistic terms, the gray, thick, overcast skies set off the fabulous colors like nowhere we had been before. As we flipped through the various scenes, the colors stood out with remarkable brilliance. The grayness of the days drew out the remarkable brilliance of the landscape.

For the most part, I hope for sunny days. Days when the warmth and power of an unobstructed sun pours full on everything I do. Days when light shines bright and brilliant on every step I take. But clouds come, rain falls, and with it a beauty emerges that the brilliance of the sun seems to dilute and overpower. It is not on the sunny days that we experience the true colors of those who stand with us, but on the cloudy ones. It is the shadows, far more than the spotlight, that expose the power and brilliance of friends and family. It is often in the gray times that we learn the most about ourselves and about life.

Life is often lived when the weather is dismal. Yet, it is the dismal weather that makes it wonderful and beautiful. Gray skies provide a perfect backdrop for full color. I have the pictures to prove it.

Have a great week.

The Orchid

It had been a long day, or maybe more accurately a short night. I'd just arrived in Munich for another series of business meetings. The procedure for these trips is now routine.

Once off the plane and through immigration, I am greeted by Kurt, the taxi driver with whom I'm in touch regularly for trips to and from the airport.

My destination from the airport is predictable as well. Most often I reside at a small German hotel within walking distance of my office. This trip was no exception. Bleary-eyed and sporting a significant five-o'clock shadow, I produced the appropriate credit card and signature on my way to room 207. When I open my hotel room door, I am greeted by familiar white walls, gray marble floors in the bathroom, and dated but clean beige carpeting. I hastily unpack my suitcase, wanting to avoid every wrinkle possible. Once my suit and shirts are hung up and my bath supplies are appropriately placed, I am ready to begin work.

On this particular trip, I noticed something new as I let myself into the room. Someone had placed a beautiful plant on the glass-topped coffee table at the far end of the room. It was a lovely orchid, two stems supporting fifteen white and purple blooms. The beauty and surprise interrupted my routine and blasted harmony through my monotone world.

All I had asked for was a clean, functional room, with a comfortable bed, a working phone, a toilet that flushes properly, and lights to illuminate my reading. I got all that, plus a burst of color and life that exceeded my expectation and provided a sense of inspiration.

In front of me was a stack of work. Mail to respond to, spreadsheets to create, presentations to prepare. They're all on my to-do list. Where do orchids fit into my daily plan? I want to do the basics well, the things that people expect of me. But after the bed is made and the bathroom is clean, I want to shop for orchids. The kind of orchids that have fifteen beautiful blooms, all perfectly opened and all saying in one clear voice, "You're important to me." I want to blast harmony into a monotone world. Orchids anyone?

Have a great week.

About the Author

Daniel S. Wolgemuth, author and motivational speaker, has been writing the Monday Memo for the past eight years. Since then, his lively commentary has touched countless lives through electronic distribution and publication in various periodicals.

In addition to his literary success, Wolgemuth serves as the Vice President of Information Technology for ERC, a division of GE Capital. He and his wife, Mary, have three children and live in Lenexa, Kansas, a suburb of Kansas City.

You may find additional information about Daniel S. Wolgemuth's weekly column by accessing the following website:

Themondaymemo.com

Additional copies of this book
are available from your local bookstore.

If you have enjoyed this book, or if it has
impacted your life, we would like to hear from you.
Please contact us at:

Honor Books
Department E
P.O. Box 55388
Tulsa, Oklahoma 74155

Or by e-mail at info@honorbooks.com